HELVETE
A JOURNAL OF BLACK METAL THEORY

Issue 1: Incipit

Winter 2013

HELVETE
A JOURNAL OF BLACK METAL THEORY
Issue 1: Incipit
Winter 2013

ISSN: 2326-683X

Helvete: A Journal of Black Metal Theory
is also available in open-access form:
http://helvetejournal.org

EDITORS
Amelia Ishmael
Zareen Price
Aspasia Stephanou
Ben Woodard

LAYOUT EDITOR
Andrew Doty

Published by
punctum books
Brooklyn, New York
http://punctumbooks.com

ISBN-13: 978-0615758282
ISBN-10: 0615758282

DILATION
EDITOR'S PREFACE

Zareen Price

The open door and gaping shadowy halls stand wide in cold splendor of marble and stone / And from pulpits appear faces that stare, cruel mockeries of the closest in life now gone[1]

This is an opening.

These are the first words, the opening text, of a project I conceived late in the winter of 2011. *Melancology*, the second iteration of the Black Metal Theory Symposium, had recently oozed through London, and the internet-lurking underground's immune reaction to the intermingling of Black Metal and theory was seemingly at its most captious. In a way, the forumites and blog commenters were right: Black Metal theory *is* an infection in danger of becoming an epidemic. Brooklyn's *Hideous Gnosis* was patient zero, and Dublin's *P.E.S.T.* has brought the count of infected to three. But these were relatively controlled environments, bounded to a particular point in space and time—*Helvete* is a metastasizing agent that threatens to spread through the venous pathways of the internet.

This is an opening. It is a tear in the skin, stretching wider and wider to expose the erstwhile sterile cavities of the body. The infection enters. But whose skin is torn? Who is the infector? Who is infected? The web is awash with a repeated answer: Black Metal theory is the infection of Black Metal by theory; it is the brutal vivisection of Black Metal's heretofore incorrupt body.

Here we have only half of one side of the wrong story. Instead, we should observe how, even if only in ideal cases, Black Metal and theory interpenetrate. They are like two questioning ichneumon wasps bonded in coital embrace, speared upon each other's alloyed ovipositors, each depositing putrefying seeds into the other's body. They are no longer individuals, but neither are they identical now that they are forcibly conjoined in nigredo. As the masthead at *Black Metal Theory* intones: "Not black metal. Not theory. Not not black metal. Not not theory."[2] Standing far from pretensions to devise some Grand Unified Theory of Black Metal, the practitioner of Black Metal theory engages in the *mutual* blackening of theory and Metal.

I open the doors to the other side and step beyond mortality[3]

With the publication of *Incipit*, I have moved from conception to pregnancy to birth. The wasps' bodies have been hollowed out as their children have glutted on organs they too are developing, and finally the larvae emerge. Like the wasps, the varied works in this volume have consumed me. My body is opened, I am poured out in print. I mingle now with the authors and artists whose texts and images follow. While critics may call this venture a hipster's fad, Ovid reminds us—and the massive redundancy of the printed and digital versions of this journal assure us—we step beyond ourselves and into the text, and the text makes us immortal. *Helvete* is the sign of a fulfilled promise: Black Metal theory will not die.

And so this is an opening. The portal gapes, and we cross from one side to the other. It is a door through which many further iterations of Black Metal theory may enter. It invites possession. In turn, possession invites metamorphosis.

Helvete, I hope, will change. My short tenure here has taught me a great deal about organizing and producing a publication. Much of this is mundane, but I expect to apply these lessons with a particular eye to publishing more works that fall outside the purview of the established academic genres. We are a para-academic journal! We should not be beholden to rigid and arbitrary norms, but rather we should use our freedom to encourage fecund experimentation. The journal's future, then, is open, awaiting only the intervention of whatever forces or unclean spirits may enter to further blacken its pages.

No beginning, no end / Words beyond words / Lead us in / Acts beyond acts[4]

Critics and supporters alike have overlooked this waiting potential, and thus they tend to approach Black Metal theory as merely the production of dense, somnolent academic texts about Black Metal. Although this is certainly an aspect of Black Metal theory, it is not the whole, as it represents only the blackening of theory by Metal—or, in the worst cases, the mere imprisonment of Metal in theory. Black Metal theory is a practice composed of many possible component practices. It is an artistic practice, a musical practice, a literary practice, a theoretical practice. When it comes to us as theory, its words are an occult intervention, the acts of theory possessed by the outsider spirit of Metal. When it comes as music, its dissonant clangs and shrieked lyrics summon forth the dark avatars of theory to haunt us. It acts—upon us, yet mostly upon itself.

Black Metal theorists reject any approach that privileges one of these practices above its fellows, and we especially refuse to countenance any call to return to the music itself. Black Metal theory is an impure practice, aiming to destroy the integrity of Metal and theory's protective membranes. There is no essence, but only an opening. Whatever demonic or unclean forces that may lodge themselves within are welcome.

Bear this in mind as you pass through this opening and move onward to the squalling pages that follow. Starve the inclination to categorize a given work of Black Metal theory as "true" or "false," and instead allow yourself to be caught up in the practice. As I have said elsewhere and seemingly in another life, the results of this experiment cannot be known in advance. Leap through the opening. Taste and see.[5]

* * *

A word or two of thanks are in order. Many, many people contributed to getting *Helvete* to print. First and foremost, I am grateful to this volume's contributors for taking a leap of faith and joining this little enterprise. The same goes for Eileen Joy and her staff at punctum books—it is a brave publisher that takes on such an offbeat project in its youth. A hearty thanks also to our editorial advisory board for their comments and suggestions, and in particular to Nicola Masciandaro for encouraging me to start the journal. Furthermore, I am indebted to my co-editors, Amelia Ishmael, Aspasia Stephanou, and Ben Woodard. Without your dedication and occasional willingness to prod me back to life, this dead mote of rock we're flying on may never have been subjected to *Helvete*. To all of you mentioned above, this journal is as much yours as it is mine—I hope you can be proud of it.

Zareen Price
Portland, 2012

NOTES
[1] Negative Plane, "Angels of Veiled Bone," *Stained Glass Revelations* (The Ajna Offensive, 2011).

[2] Nicola Masciandaro, *Black Metal Theory*, http://blackmetaltheory.blogspot.com. Details about all three Black Metal theory symposia mentioned above can also be found here.

[3] Abigor, "Utopia Consumed," *Channeling the Quintessence of Satan* (Napalm Records, 1999).

[4] Dødsengel, "Towers of Derinkuyu," *Imperator* (Barghest and Terratur Possessions, 2012).

[5] Zareen Price, "You Were Talking About a Black Metal Theory; What the Fuck Is That!!!," *The Lichenthrope*, April 4, 2011, http://thelichenthrope.blogspot.com/2011/04/you-were-talking-about-black-metal.html.

OPEN A VEIN
SUICIDAL BLACK METAL AND ENLIGHTENMENT[1]

Janet Silk

Black Metal was born in suicide. The image of Per Yngve Ohlin (aka Dead) on the 1995 album cover of Mayhem's *Dawn of the Black Hearts*, his blown-out brains oozing out of his shattered skull, is an icon that foreshadowed the emergence of Suicidal Black Metal (SBM) bands who skirt the edge between ideation and action.[2] For bands such as Shining, Make a Change . . . Kill Yourself, and I Shalt Become, suicide and self-harm are cathexes; death is the ultimate life lesson—we must reflect on it, embrace it . . . and do it. Albert Camus articulates in *The Myth of Sisyphus*, "There is but one truly serious philosophical problem and that is suicide."[3] Within the broad spectrum of philosophical positions which Black Metal represents (such as nihilism, existentialism, satanism, and abjection) is SBM's celebration of self-destruction. What might be the function of this celebration?

Enlightenment is often described as an awakening of consciousness that is sustained. It is a station or place of insightful awareness about the nature of reality. The Sanskrit and Pali word *bodhi* means "awakened," and within many Buddhist practices this state can be activated through meditation on death.[4] Partial self-burial (digging and sleeping in one's own open grave) and forcing oneself to gaze upon a corpse are classic death awareness practices.[5] As we contemplate our mortality, we may come to understand the meaning of our existence. By extension, suicide is the ancient playground where each individual can explore and contest his or her own death. As Arthur Schopenhauer states: "Suicide may also be regarded as an experiment—a question which man puts to Nature, trying to force her to answer. The question is this: What change will death produce in a man's existence and in his insight into the nature of things?"[6] From this perspective, an individual who struggles with or decides to suicide has the potential to attain self-knowledge, wisdom, and purpose.

Accounts of enlightenment are infused with transcendental and ecstatic language. For example, Evelyn Underhill in *Mysticism* introduces terms such as Absolute Reality, The Transcendental World, and Undifferentiated Life. Aldous Huxley, in *The Doors of Perception*, writes of the Clear Light of the Void, the Inner Light, and Unmitigated Reality.[7] Other expressions use "light" metaphors such as "to see the light," "to gaze on ten suns shining," "to be surrounded in white light," "to be guided by the light," or to encounter whitening, flashing, ebbing light. So, although Shining's vocalist Niklas Kvarforth denies any specific religious topic in the band's music, it is significant that he has described the band's name to mean "the path to enlightenment."[8] Also, Kvarforth claims that he started to explore destroying himself physically and psychologically at a very young stage in his life, in order "to break all the borders and to fuck myself up to get to a higher level."[9] This is analogous to many hierarchically organized spiritual traditions where a person strives to attain enlightenment in stages, often through a series of particular practices or exercises which may involve self-inflicted physical pain, self-denial, and self-torture.

According to James Hillman, author of *Suicide and the Soul*, self-knowledge is the essential motivation for suicide. He states, "Suicide is pre-judged by the medical mode of thought . . . it can be understood medically only as a symptom, an aberration, an alienation, to be approached with the point of view of prevention."[10] Rather than negate suicide as pathology, he asks what it means to the psyche; he believes that suicide is an attempt to transform the soul. The drive to kill oneself is really a demand for an encounter with absolute reality—a demand for a profound overthrow of daily life.

This encounter requires planning and rehearsal. Sitting quietly one visualizes the scene: the right outfit, the lighting, and the ambience. What will the note say? What tools are needed? Is the bar in the closet high enough? Rope or wire? Razor blades are messy, but cutting is seductively and strangely appealing, and seeing one's own blood is intoxicating. By replaying and rewriting the scene, one exerts control over one's death. Suicide is an escape clause in the contract of life, a free zone where one can reject or affirm death. By playing with the choice to live or die, each moment is ripe with meaning. As Camus states, "Judging whether life is or is not worth living amounts to answering the fundamental question of philosophy."[11] The suicidal person wants to use death for a purpose. This search for purpose becomes ground zero for divergent revolutionary acts, many supported by an ideology that accepts self-killing as a spiritual or mystical event and as evidence of one's altruism. Some practices within Mahayana Buddhism, Islam, and Christianity tolerate an individual's choice for self-annihilation for various reasons including political protest, sacrificial devotion, and contemplative renunciation.[12]

In protest against the Ngô Đình Diệm administration's persecution of Buddhists, on June 11, 1963, the South Vietnamese Mahayana Buddhist monk Thích Quảng Đức burned himself to death in the middle of a busy Saigon road intersection. His self-immolation garnered worldwide media coverage and exacerbated the downfall of the Diệm regime. However, Thích Quảng Đức's action was not unprecedented. Historically, ordinary men and women, as well as monks and nuns, have embraced self-immolation for both political protest and in order to honor Guatama Buddha.[13] One aspect of Mahayana Buddhism is that, besides self-liberation, it is important for followers to help other sentient beings. In this context, burning oneself is an act of sacrifice and love for the greater good of humanity. Self-destructive actions are reframed according to a person's compassionate intention.

Another more recent incidence of self-immolation occurred in Tunisia on December 17, 2010, when Mohamed Bouazizi, an unemployed, college graduate who was trying to work as a street vendor, set himself on fire as a result of his frustration with the municipal officers who had harassed him and confiscated his wares. Bouazzi's desperate action is credited as the catalyst for violent country-wide protests against President Zine al-Abidine Ben Ali's government, which forced Ben Ali and his family to flee the country a month later. The Tunisian uprising served as inspiration for demonstrations and revolutions that have spread throughout the Middle East. After Bouazizi's suicide, a wave of copycat self-immolations continues to bloom, adding a tone of bloody pathos to what is often cheerily referred to as "The Arab Spring" or "The Arab Awakening."[14]

Suicide bombing is a fusion of offering up one's life for a cause and forcing people to wake up to an oppressive reality. Wilhelm Stekel (Austrian physician, psychologist, and student of Freud) remarked, "No one kills himself who has never wanted to kill another, or at least wished the death of another."[15] Wishing for the death of a particular person or group, the suicide bomber rages against the social injustice inflicted by the enemy. The bomber is both victim and murderer and paradoxically screams, "I'll die and then you'll be sorry." The hope is to survive—if not in body, then in spirit—and to witness the enemy's suffering. The Palestinian Sunni Islamic political party Hamas (an Arabic word for "zeal" or "enthusiasm") has long advocated suicide bombings. Recruits are assured their place in Paradise and revered as martyrs after their death. The blood of martyrs lights the way, and Hamas's rhetoric is imbued with admonitions that words remain dead until people are willing to die for the cause. The famed Palestinian Islamist Abdullah Yusuf Azzam writes, "Glory does not build its lofty edifice except with skulls; honor and respect cannot be established except on a foundation of cripples and corpses."[16] Those who enlist as *shaheeds* (martyrs) imagine the laudations after the bombing mission, fantasize about the respect and reverence that will be lavished on their families, and hope to be role models for others on the path to glory.

Potential suicide bombers describe a sense of elation or of being uplifted when he or she decides to become a *shaheed* or *shaheeda*. There is an ecstatic camaraderie in the face of death—each bomber knowing that he or she will take his or her place on the roster of great Martyrs—and death is a kind of trophy. A *shaheed* rehearses his death lovingly, as many times as possible, and reflects on it with serene happiness. Not unlike an ascetic spiritual exercise, a mock burial may be performed and a would-be martyr may be temporarily interred in an empty grave, either alone or with comrades.[17] A feeling of renewal is earned by overcoming the natural fear of death, and many suicide survivors report a feeling of clarity and even a renewed zest for life.[18] As explained by Shafiqa, a failed suicide bomber, "It took me a long time to decide . . . It was wonderful to say good-bye to life. I felt like I was up in the clouds from the moment I knew I was going to be a shaheeda."[19] According to Hamas, there are plenty of people enthusiastically enlisting for the opportunity to blow themselves up, and they insist that they only recruit people who are "normal"—not suicidal or depressed. Suicide bombers must have pure motives, open hearts, and a desire for Allah.[20]

Muhammad Atta is considered the ringleader of the September 11, 2001 terrorist attacks against the United States. His infamous document "The Last Night" is a series of reminders to his comrades, mostly prescriptions and quotations from the Qur'an, Islamic Shari'ah Law, and Sunnah (teachings from the life of Muhammad).[21] Ritualistic traditions are recommended along each step of the last journey, such as the need to shave body hair and wear cologne, to have sharpened knives, to make sure one's privates are covered, to wear proper socks and shoes, to think well of one's brothers, to pray and remember Allah in the taxi and airplane, and to make sure that the hostages are slaughtered comfortably (as is the practice for Islamic animal slaughter known as *dhabihah*). It also shares advice that, in the end, it is imperative to be calm and optimistic:

> You should feel complete tranquility, because the time between you and your marriage [in heaven] is very short. Afterwards begins the happy life, where God is satisfied with you, and eternal bliss in the company of the prophets, the companions, the martyrs and the good people, who are all good company. Ask God for his mercy and be optimistic, because [the Prophet], peace be upon him, used to prefer optimism in all his affairs.[22]

These statements are like those from an enlightenment-seeking aspirant who hopes to arrive at a happy, calm, and expansive state.

There are many examples of religious martyrs (Dead has been called a rock-star martyr) who seek heightened states of consciousness and recondite lifestyles; they urge humanity to find authenticity in a sea of illusions.[23] This condemnation of the material world—in contrast to the laudation of a luminous heaven or the veneration of an illuminated altered state—can be found in many spiritual ideologies, some pitting the body against the soul or spirit: the fleshy body becomes subject to mutilation and destruction for the sake of some higher purpose. The central figure of Christianity, Jesus Christ, is a perfect example of this; his submission to crucifixion and torture for the sake of humanity's salvation was the penultimate sacrifice that birthed a religion.[24] Later, so many willing martyrs followed his example that the Church fathers became concerned and debated the ethics of suicide for three centuries.[25] Christianity, like Islam, teaches that earthly existence is a grim prelude to the fantastical, psychedelic, exalted world that greets believers after they die; this certainly offers an incentive for martyrdom, or at least makes sacrificial self-killing an honorable option.[26] Through martyrdom a person becomes holy; the act can be both purifying and revolutionary.

The martyr's theater reveals the benefits of self-mutilation and the rewards for choosing physical or spiritual death in order to attain something grander than life. Through his masochistic self-torture, Saint Simeon Stylites (one of the most famous *stylitoe*, or "pillar-hermits") set an example for chronic suicide as a road to spiritual advancement. He stood on one leg for a year, atop a sixty-foot pillar that was exposed to the elements, while the other leg mushroomed into sores filled with pus and worms. Saint Simeon would ask people to put any fallen worms back in, coaxing the worms to "eat what God has given you."[27] Gustave Flaubert's Saint Anthony boasted, "those who are decapitated, tortured with red hot pincers, or burned alive, are perhaps less meritorious than I, seeing that my whole life is but one prolonged martyrdom."[28] There are numerous accounts of Christians who begged to be martyred throughout the history of ancient Rome. Because death was only of the body, not of the soul, they would rush to the pagan judges, proclaiming their faith, and when sentenced, they would hold hands and sing as they faced the lions in the Colosseum. The crowd bears witness to the passion of Christian faith, ennobling its creed, and inspiring believers. The Christian martyr conquers death—the body is only a means to an end, a vehicle for the martyr's desires.

SBM's themes, such as self-mutilation and the renunciation of life, relate to some of the ascendant aspirations of religious suicide. Make a Change . . . Kill Yourself invites the listener:

My great salvation lies within
This suicidal mind of mine.
Join me in this wicked state of suicide.[29]

This renunciation reflects concepts in Buddhism, Islam, and Christianity that cast doubt upon the benefit of the corporeal world. In several Hindu and Buddhist traditions, *maya* is defined as the alluringly hypnotic, superficial illusion of physical reality, and the goal is to break the spell and to realize numinous truth.[30] Existence on earth is ephemeral, the body temporary, and biological life is not only meaningless but filled with suffering. Death is also the point of contact with the eternal.[31] In Islam, the Arabic word *dunya* means "lower" and connotes all that is worldly and temporal. The *dunya* may be beautiful and pleasurable, but it is fleeting, and it is better to turn one's gaze on what is immutable. Everything is a test that can lead to paradise or hell. The Qur'an is clear: "Nay (behold), you prefer the life of this world; but the Hereafter is better and more enduring."[32] Christianity warns against sinful worldliness: "Do not love the world or anything in the world."[33] This sentiment is echoed in Shining's lyrics "Through Corridors of Oppression":

Slowly,
passing the oppressed,
innocent,
sons,
and daughters lost,
trembling
in the bottomless depths of darkness,
successfully,
failing
in their search.

To search
the light,
to search,
salvation.[34]

Self-destruction or self-harm opposes the ego's natural inclination for self-preservation (physically and experientially) and serves as a testament to a person's non-attachment to illusory life: one destroys oneself, and in doing so one destroys the world.[35] This connects with psychoanalytic theories by James Hillman, which argue that the drive to kill oneself is a demand for the profound overthrow of daily life.[36] The music paints a putrid existence, and charges that the world is a perpetual, degenerative "whore" (according to Ondskapt's vocalist Acerbus) who lures humanity into ever-deeper levels of hellish darkness and violence.[37] SBM is a mirror and creative response to the misery.

Suicide is murder. The American psychiatrist Karl Menninger believed that there are three elements necessary in order for someone to commit suicide: the wish to kill, the wish to be killed, and the wish to die.[38] In *Man Against Himself*, Menninger writes, "There is a little murder and a little suicide dwelling in everybody's heart."[39] Kvarforth asserts that the whole objective of Shining is to teach people to destroy themselves, or to force-feed people with self-destructive and suicidal imagery and lyrics. The aim of the band is to hurt, to give birth to future psychopaths and a breed of people who believe in the destruction of mankind. He prescribes an end to the polymorphous perverse, obscenely pulsating overabundance of life. Kvarforth states:

> I hate life and I hate living, I truly, truly hate life in all its fucking perverse forms . . . animals, nature, everything that grows must be put to death. But that's just fantasies. I think that mankind is pretty good at fucking ourselves up in a way, you know, but if I can push it a little bit it's good.[40]

In the documentary video *Black Metal Satanica*, he describes the thrill he experienced when he accidentally cut open someone's arm, revealing the bone, and also how he cut someone's leg open, took out a piece of flesh, and tried to "feed a whore" who was standing nearby (a performance that he compared to the Catholic Holy Communion ritual).[41] Kvarforth is notorious for passing out razor blades at concerts. He combines cannibalistic priestly gestures, ritualistic self-mutilations, and apocalyptic, anti-life sermons to exterminate hopeful dreams and floating world illusions.[42]

> A suicidal haze, unreal like a torturous dream
> Old stinging mental wounds, still raw and fucking bleeding
> Drowning in the womb of misery, the mother of depression
> The slaughter of all hope, the grim death of compassion
> Sell your soul to evil; sell your soul to death
> . . . Suicide, suicide, suicide, suicide, suicide, suicide, suicide . . .
> A dead empty stare into the ruins of my world
> A world I have already left, so many years ago[43]

It is as Nietzsche elucidated: "hope,—in reality it is the worst of all evils, because it prolongs the torments of man."[44]

These musicians, like the literary artists Antonin Artaud and Yukio Mishima, consider suicide an achievement. Artaud confides:

If I commit suicide, it will not be to destroy myself but to put myself back together again. Suicide will be for me only one means of violently reconquering myself, of brutally invading my being, of anticipating the unpredictable approaches of God. By suicide, I reintroduce my design in nature; I shall for the first time give things the shape of my will.[45]

Through suicide a person triumphs over the mundane, common, and ugly; a person is most heroic when he or she is unafraid of ending his or her life.

In Japan, an orchestrated self-killing is tolerated and considered an action of honor and respect. Historically, *seppuku*, or *hari-kiri* ("belly-cutting"), developed from the military class and was a revered form of suicide and a purification ritual. Whether voluntary or obligatory, the climax of the ceremony is death by self-disembowelment: a left to right slice deep in the belly, and a final beheading by a specially trained swordsman. Opening up the abdomen symbolizes that the center of the person's being is undefiled.[46] Author Yukio Mishima criticized the moral and material decadence imported into Japan from the West, championing a return to traditions of Imperial Japan and the samurai code of conduct.[47] He was obsessed with *seppuku*. Hoping to restore the code of the samurai, he created the Shield Society, a private army of eighty-five men, which Mishima described as "the world's least armed, most spiritual army."[48] On November 25, 1970, Mishima and four Shield Society members raided and seized the Tokyo-based Ichigaya Military Headquarters of Japan's Self-Defense Forces. From a balcony, he gave a confrontational and provocative speech, imploring the crowd of 200 servicemen to return to the traditional ways of Imperial Japan. Mishima admonished that the Japanese thought only of money and had no patriotic or spiritual foundation.[49] After his speech, which was not well received, he walked back inside the Headquarters and committed *seppuku*. His *kaishaku* (suicide assistant) completed the ritual with Mishima's beheading, which partly failed when the *kaishaku* tried three times to sever the head from the body before one of Mishima's other acolytes was finally successful.[50] Now legendary, the coup and ritualized suicide was ridiculed at the time, yet is emblematic of Mishima's idealization of samurai morality and of his exaltation of suicide as an aesthetic act, a way to preserve the beauty of youth: "If you want your beauty to endure you must commit suicide at the height of your beauty."[51] Throughout his life, Mishima desired to be not just a man of letters and words but "a man of action," and in order to reclaim his honor he followed a paradigm of ferocious self-destruction. On the appointed day, he submitted the last pages of his last book to his publisher and composed his death poem:

A small night storm blows
Saying "falling is the essence of a flower"

Then those who hesitate arrived.[52]

Dead is legendary for declaring his stance against the trendiness and commercialism of the Extreme Metal (in particular, Death Metal) scene of his time. Bands like Mayhem sought a radically evil, dark, and aggressive sound, and more bloody, transgressive, and theatrical stage shows.[53] The origins of the Black Metal scene came from a disillusionment with mediocrity, commercialism, and poserdom; bands needed the will to make the violent and destructive content of the music real.[54] This challenge to the mainstream is what drove band members and fans beyond the taboos around self-murder, homicide, vandalism, and arson. As the sociologist Keith Kahn-Harris writes in *Extreme Metal: Music and Culture on the Edge*, "Transgression, like extremity, implies a sense of testing and crossing boundaries and limits." He continues, "Ultimately, transgression is dangerous" and "both dissolves and affirms being."[55] Transgressive behavior is empowering in that it declares war on social norms, authority, and the law. In terms of suicide, scholars of self-destruction (such as Hillman) argue for a morally neutral and positive hermeneutical approach to the problem: culturally sanctioned attitudes do exist, if not for the act itself, then for its philosophical, spiritual, and political significance. This is the terrain of SBM.

SBM abounds with the transformative possibilities in contemplating and determining one's own death. This position is explicitly literal in the name of the band Make A Change . . . Kill Yourself. Band member Ynleborgaz explains that he received "some suicide letters" in the summer of 2004 that inspired him to "discover a whole new world inside his head" and to create "desolate landscapes of depressive melodies."[56] He (along with lyricist Nattetale) used the letters as a catalyst to explore the "darkest side of his psyche"[57]:

> . . . As I drop lifeless to the floor.
> Follow my footprints of blood: my steps of blood.
> Leave everything behind you and step into my reality.
> Where no happiness is found.
> Feel the wind torment your skin.
> Feel the sun burn your skin and turn to stone.
> Feel my razor blades tongue and cut yourself deep and desirably.
> Let the blood run in an overflowing stream and submit to my suicide and yours.
> Nothing but death in this life is certain.
> You may be in some state of happiness but none of this will stay real.
> You are trapped in a spider's web.
> You might as well just kill yourself.[58]

Make A Change . . . Kill Yourself reminds listeners of their own mortality, the fragility of life, and the transitory nature of happiness. However, in spite of the music being a liminal space in which to play with controversial themes and language, writers such as Harris and the theologian Jason Forster critique those aspects of the Extreme Metal genre that champion death and destruction simply to shock people and sell records. From this perspective, musicians who just "talk the talk" are fakes, in contrast to a musician like Dead, a man of action, who followed the ideology to its logical conclusion. Developing this idea further (even though their actions are in a different context), suicide bombers, self-immolating monks and street vendors, and self-disemboweling writers are true SBM artists. As Camus reflected, "An act like this is prepared within the silence of the heart, as is a great work of art."[59]

Euronymous's photo of Dead on the cover of Mayhem's *Dawn of the Black Hearts* is a visual representation of a complex discourse between music as an agent for individual edification or social change, and music as entertainment. It is a seminal relic of the violent, death-worshipping origin of Black Metal, and an icon for those who continue to play with its symbolic inversion of normative values in order to be innovative and revolutionary.[60] The fundamental aesthetics of the scene have been reproduced by thousands of bands who showcase real and staged actions, and project images of self-mutilation and self-destruction, in order to provoke the audience out of their contented apathy and from what Ernest Hemingway referred to as "backing into the grave."[61] Suicidogenic heroes and heroines celebrate the pleasure of having the option to choose death, and with it the joy of discovering that a person must cast away his or her life in order to live. Joy is a recurrent theme in the accounts of suicide survivors and in the rich and varied ideas found in suicidological literature. In George Howe Colt's *November of the Soul: the Enigma of Suicide*, a twenty-five-year-old man is quoted who makes clear the triumph he felt when he decided to take his own life:

> It was like being in class and everyone around you is giving the wrong answer . . . Blowing your head off is the answer. The answer to life, the answer to your identity, the answer to your self-preservation. That gun to your head is the most beautiful answer. And even as you are thinking of killing yourself, you can be full of passion, full of life. I think for many people it's that zest to live that makes them keep wrapping the noose around their neck. They're saying, "I'll show you how much I want to live."[62]

How many people slowly suffocate themselves in customs, habits, and apathy? The end of inquisitive curiosity and expansive speculation is an early intrusion of death. For I Shalt Become, suicide is a way to break away from this smothering blanket of uninspired lethargy:

A last, choked breath
Before lifelessly
The body hangs

A cheer rises from the crowd
A sway in the breeze
And life continues.[63]

Even though the imagery and content of SBM's music may be morbid and shockingly painful, it is purposefully invested in the venerable quest to maintain human dignity.

No single theory can elucidate the complex motives for suicide. However, it is vital to remember that in the above lyrics for "End Time" the crowd happily cheers as the veil is lifted between this world and the next, and that the actor has a receptive audience, no matter how disturbing the end game. There is admiration and respect for those who overcome the body's "will to live" and those who choose to be masters of their fate.[64] There is pleasure in remembering one's freedom to choose death, or at least the freedom to choose between available options. Suicide notes and statements by survivors often express the clarity of the Chosen Death: the suicide bomber, for example, may find more satisfaction from determining the day and method of his or her own death than the person who clings so passionately to life. But it is not enough to just die; one's death must have a purpose. The vehement examples discussed here illustrate motivations such as release, revolution, revenge, and ritual purification. The distinct focus of Suicidal Black Metal traces these multifarious answers to the suicide question: the listener is immersed in an atmosphere that resonates with both the pleasure and the pain of self-destruction; veins are slashed open to insist that one is very much alive. As Dead's suicide note wryly ends: "Excuse all the blood. Let the party begin."[65]

NOTES

[1]   Open a vein
To watch it . . .
It fits in
Too much it . . .

Disinvite
Dis-disinvite
Disinvite
When I'm looking alone
Trying alone

Melvins, "Disinvite," *Gluey Porch Treatments* (Alchemy Records, 1986). All lyrics throughout essay cited from *Encyclopaedia Metallum: The Metal Archives*, http://www.metal-archives.com.

[2] Also referred to as Depressive Suicidal Black Metal (DSBM).

[3] Albert Camus, *The Myth of Sisyphus* (Harmondsworth: Penguin, 1980), 11. In conclusion, Camus rejects suicide both philosophically and physically, and he explains that the task of living should be accepted. In contrast to this position, this essay presents ideas that are in favor of the individual's right to choose suicide and possible motivations for choosing suicide. See Beatriz Scaglia's "Philosophy of Suicide," in *On Fire for a Cause: The Horror of Self-Immolation* (Webster's Digital Services, 2011), 47. See also, Michael Cholbi, "Libertarian Views and the Right to Suicide" in "Suicide," 3.4, *Stanford Encyclopedia of Philosophy*, July 29, 2008, http://plato.stanford.edu/entries/suicide.

[4] Also referred to as *marananussati bhavana*, see V.F. Gunaratna, "Buddhist Reflections on Death," *Access to Insight: Readings in Theravada Buddhism* 1994-2011, http://www.accesstoinsight.org/lib/authors/gunaratna/wheel102.html. No doubt this statement about Buddhist thought is a generalization and deserves a more nuanced presentation, however the author has limited the examples for the sake of brevity. Consider this poem by Zen Master Hakuin Ekaku:

> The monkey is reaching
> For the moon in the water.
> Until death overtakes him
> He'll never give up.
> If he'd let go the branch and
> Disappeared in the deep pool,
> The whole world would shine
> With dazzling pureness.

[5] See Larry Rosenburg's account of how his teacher led a meditation in the same room of a decaying corpse. Rosenburg, "The Supreme Meditation," *Shambala Sun*, November 2000, http://www.shambhalasun.com/index.php?option=content&task=view&id=1792.

[6] Arthur Schopenhauer, "On Suicide," in *Studies in Pessimism* (New York: Cosimo, 2007), 29.

[7] Marghanita Laski, *Ecstasy in Secular and Religious Experiences* (London: Cresset Press, 1961), 240.

[8] Mats Lundberg, *Black Metal Satanica*, DVD (Cleopatra, 2008). Interview with Kvarforth by *Black Terror Webzine* (October 2005), quoted in "Interviews," *Shining*, http://shiningband.tripod.com/interviews-blackterror.html.

[9] Lundberg, *Black Metal Satanica*.

[10] James Hillman, *Suicide and the Soul*, quoted in George Howe Colt, *November of the Soul: The Enigma of Suicide* (New York: Summit Books, 1991), 343–344.

[11] Camus, *The Myth of Sisyphus*, 11.

[12] These altruistic virtues are not limited to religious discourse; however, the author is using examples from three religious traditions for the purposes of exploring the language used to describe spiritual enlightenment.

[13] Colt, *November of the Soul*, 235. The twenty-third chapter of the *Lotus Sutra* is reported to have been the inspiration for the monks and nuns who self-immolated to protest the Vietnam War. The chapter tells the story of the Medicine King Bodhisattva who burned himself as an offering to Buddha.

[14] See "Arab Spring," *Wikipedia: The Free Encyclopedia*, http://en.wikipedia.org/wiki/Arab_Spring. See also Josh Sanburn, "A Brief History of Self-Immolation," *Time*, January 20, 2011, http://www.time.com/time/world/article/0,8599,2043123,00.html.

[15] Al Alvarez, *The Savage God* (New York: Random House, 1971), 103.

[16] Ann Marie Oliver and Paul F. Steinberg, *The Road to Martyrs' Square: A Journey into the World of the Suicide Bomber* (New York: Oxford University Press, 2005), xxi.

[17] Oliver and Steinberg, *The Road to Martyrs' Square*, 75.

[18] Alvarez, *The Savage God*, 100. See also Steve Taylor, *Durkheim and the Study of Suicide* (London: Macmillan, 1982), 150–153.

[19] Anat Berko, *The Path to Paradise: The Inner World of Suicide Bombers and Their Dispatchers* (Westport: Praeger Security International, 2007), 118.

[20] Oliver and Steinberg, *The Road to Martyrs' Square*, 119.

[21] "Last Words of a Terrorist," *The Guardian*, September 30, 2011, http://www.guardian.co.uk/world/2001/sep/30/terrorism.september113.

[22] "Last Words of a Terrorist."

[23] It is interesting to note that the English word *martyr* derives from the Greek word "witness" (*martys*) and that the Arabic words for martyr and witness (*shaheed*) are identical. The martyr's gift of self-sacrifice is intimately tied with a public witnessing (by either people or supernatural beings) of the event: see Keith Lewinstein, "The Revaluation of Martyrdom in Early Islam," in Margaret Cormack, ed. *Sacrificing the Self: Perspectives on Martyrdom and Religion* (New York: Oxford University Press, 2002), 78-79. Consider also at a concert how the audience witnesses staged self-mutilation by frontmen such as the Shining's Kvarforth: Joseph Allen, "'Dead' on His Last Album Cover," *Rock Star Martyr*, April 8, 2011, http://rockstarmartyr.net/dead-on-his-last-album-cover/. While the term authenticity has been challenged by postmodern cultural theorists, it is used here as a term to describe a state of being in the world in accordance with the truth and reality of one's sense of self. See "Authenticity," *New World Encyclopedia*, www.newworldencyclopedia.org/entry/Authenticity_(philosophy).

[24] 1 Corinthians 15: 54–55. Apostle Paul proclaims that Christians need not fear death because of Christ's sacrificial atonement for humanity's sins: "Death is swallowed up in victory. O death, where is thy sting? O grave where is thy victory?" The soul is victorious.

[25] George Minois, *History of Suicide: Voluntary Death in Western Culture* (Baltimore: John Hopkins University Press, 1999), 26.

[26] Carlin Barton, "Honor and Sacredness in the Roman and Christian Worlds," in Cormack, *Sacrificng the Self*, 30. The etymology of the word sacrifice includes the Latin word *sacrificare*, 'holy-making,' its root meaning *sacra*, 'sacred rights.'

[27] Colt, *November of the Soul*, 155.

[28] Gustave Flaubert, *The Temptation of Saint Anthony*, quoted in Cormack, *Sacrificing the Self*, 155.

[29] Make a Change . . . Kill Yourself, "Chapter III," *Make a Change . . . Kill Yourself* (Total Holocaust Records, 2005).

[30] "Maya (Buddhism)," *Knowledge Rush*, http://www.knowledgerush.com/kr/encyclopedia/Maya_(Buddhism). See also Jason Forster, "Commodified Evil's Wayward Children: Black Metal and Death Metal as Purveyors of an Alternative Form of Modern Escapism" (PhD diss., University of Canterbury, 2006), 82; http://ir.canterbury.ac.nz/bitstream/10092/966/1/thesis_fulltext.pdf.

[31] Colt, *November of the Soul*, 137.

[32] Sûrah al-A`lâ: 16–17.

[33] 1 John 2: 15–17.

[34] Shining, "Through Corridors of Oppression," *Through Years of Oppression* (Unexploded Records, 2004).

[35] Colt, *November of the Soul*, 226.

[36] See, for example, James Hillman, *Suicide and the Soul* (Woodstock: Spring Publications, 1997).

[37] In Lundberg's video documentary *Black Metal Satanica*, Acerbus from the Black Metal band Ondskapt comments on why his music might be just a pale reflection of the diabolical nature of everyday life: "I can tell you this, that if this whore of a world lasts even ten more years you'll find something even heavier than Ondskapt. I can tell you that something more advanced, something more devilish, more extreme . . . I don't know if it will be raping babies or if it would be burning priests on local television . . . I don't know if it would be some kind of genocide which is filmed for the camera."

[38] Colt, *November of the Soul*, 201.

[39] Karl Menninger, *Man Against Himself*, quoted in Colt, *November of the Soul*, 271.

[40] Lundberg, *Black Metal Satanica*.

[41] Lundberg, *Black Metal Satanica*.

[42] The Japanese word *ukiyo* is literally translated in English as "floating world." It means a world of impermanent, fleeting beauty and amusement. A genre of Japanese painting developed during the 17th to the 19th centuries that portrayed the world of kabuki, courtesans, and geisha, all divorced from the responsibilities of the mundane, everyday world: "Definition of Ukiyo-e," *Babylon*, http://dictionary.babylon.com/ukiyo-e.

[43] Shining, "Claws of Perdition," *Album IV: The Eerie Cold* (Avantgarde Music, 2005).

[44] Fredrik Nietzsche, *Human, All Too Human* (Neeland Media, 2010), 42.

[45] Antonin Artaud "On Suicide," quoted in Colt, *November of the Soul*, 226.

[46] David Chidester, *Salvation and Suicide: An Interpretation of Jim Jones, the Peoples Temple, and Jonestown* (Bloomington and Indianapolis: Indiana University Press, 1988), 133.

[47] Chidester, *Salvation and Suicide*, 141.

[48] "Yukio Mishima," *Philosopedia*, http://philosopedia.org/index.php/Yukio_Mishima.

[49] "Yukio Mishima," *Philosopedia*.

[50] "November 25, 1970," *The Yukio Mishima Web Page*, ed. Dennis Michael Iannuzzi, http://www.members.tripod.com/dennismichaeliannuzz/finalDay.html. See also Colt, *November of the Soul*, 141.

[51] Yukio Mishima, quoted in Colt, *November of the Soul*, 141. Consider the famous line said by actor John Derek in the film *Knock on Any Door* (1949): "Live fast, die young and have a good-looking corpse!"

[52] Carlos Mal, "The Death Poem of Mishima," *No More Mr. Nice Poet*, July 30, 2009, http://nomoremisternicepoet.blogspot.com/2009/07/death-poem-of-mishima.html.

[53] Michael Moynihan and Didrik Søderlind, *Lords of Chaos: The Bloody Rise of the Satanic Metal Underground* (Los Angeles: Feral House, 2003), 58–62.

[54] Forster, "Commodified Evil's Wayward Children," 24–28.

[55] Keith Kahn-Harris, *Extreme Metal: Music and Culture on the Edge* (New York: Berg, 2007), 29.

[56] Robert Sun, "Interview: Make A Change . . . Kill Yourself," *Mirgilus Siculorum*, May 2008, http://www.mirgilus.com/interviews/macky.html.

[57] HansKopf, "Interview with Ynleborgaz (Make A Change . . . Kill Yourself, Angantyr, Blodarv)," *Mortem Zine*, January 31, 2007, http://www.mortemzine.net/show.php?id=453.

[58] Make a Change . . . Kill Yourself, "Chapter II," *Make a Change . . . Kill Yourself* (Total Holocaust Records, 2005).

[59] Alvarez, *The Savage God*, 99.

[60] "Years later, Necrobutcher spoke of the impact of Per Yngve Ohlin's icon: 'Some people became more aware of the scene after Dead had shot himself. After that, churches started to burn and it just went crazy here. I think it was Dead's suicide that really changed the whole scene. . . . A lot of young musicians got into the scene because it was the most aggressive and violent scene out there at the time'": Allen, "'Dead' on His Last Album Cover."

[61] Ernest Hemingway, quoted in Colt, *November of the Soul*, 271.

[62] Colt, *November of the Soul*, 228.

[63] I Shalt Become, "End Time," *The Pendle Witch Trials* (No Colours Records, 2009).

[64] Schopenhauer, *Studies in Pessimism*: "It will generally be found that, as soon as the terrors of life reach the point at which they outweigh the terrors of death, a man will put an end to his own life. But the terrors of death offer considerable resistance; they stand like a sentinel at the gate leading out of this world. Perhaps there is no man alive who would not have already put an end to his own life, if this end had been of a purely negative character, a sudden stoppage of existence. There is something positive about it; it is the destruction of the body; and a man shrinks from that, because his body is the manifestation of the will to live" (29).

See also William Ernest Henley's "Invictus," (1875):

Black as the Pit from pole to pole,
I thank whatever gods may be
For my unconquerable soul.

In the fell clutch of circumstance
I have not winced nor cried aloud.
Under the bludgeoning of chance
My head is bloody, but unbowed.

Beyond this place of wrath and tears
Looms but the Horror of the shade,
And yet the menace of the years
Finds, and shall find, me unafraid.

It matters not how strait the gate,
How charged with punishments the scroll.
I am the master of my fate:
I am the captain of my soul.

[65] There are different reported versions of Dead's final statement. See Chris Campion, "In the Face of Death," *The Guardian*, February 20, 2005, http://www.guardian.co.uk/music/2005/feb/20/popandrock4; Moynihan and Søderlind, *Lords of Chaos*, 62; and "Biography," *Pell Yngve Ohlin*, http://www.freewebs.com/peryngveohlin/Pages/Biography.html.

AT THE EDGE OF THE SMOKING POOL OF DEATH
WOLVES IN THE THRONE ROOM

Timothy Morton

In a rich and extensive interview, the Black Metal band Wolves in the Throne Room argue that the age of ecology is an age of hypocrisy:

> One of the many contradictions of Black Metal is that it is a music that decries civilization, but relies on so many modern contrivances to exist. I don't think it is a natural sound at all. It is really the sound of paradox, ambiguity, confusion, being caught between two worlds that cannot be reconciled. I have had people throw this in my face before—"how can you play music that is supposedly anti-civilization on electric guitars?" Frankly I find this line of reason boring and pointless. I remember a common line against rioters trashing the Nike store in downtown Seattle. There was a famous picture of some black-clad kid smashing the Nike sign, but zoom in and . . . ah-haa!! He's wearing Nike sneakers! I say, who fucking cares? Catharsis is our objective, not a lily-white and guilt free existence. We are all hypocrites and failures. [1]

This very suggestive statement resonates powerfully with what I take to be the *time of hyperobjects*, a historical moment in which nonhumans make decisive and irreversible contact with humans, within the discourses of rationalism, empiricism, and science. Of course, these contacts and affiliations have existed throughout the history of the human species, and some cultures have acknowledged them more potently than others. But the time of hyperobjects makes it impossible for *anyone, anywhere,* not to be affected by nonhumans.

The notion of hypocrisy is based on the fact of being trapped inside a gigantic entity, or a series of them, like Jonah in the Whale. I argue that Wolves in the Throne Room perform this entrapment in their version of Metal. By creating sonic hyperobjects, the music of Wolves in the Throne Room is highly congruent with the contemporary social and political situation. Moreover, as allies of the environmental advocacy group Earth First!, Wolves in the Throne Room have performed a very significant distortion of normative environmentalist subjectivity, also related to their assumption that, "Against the hyperobject we are always in the wrong," to adapt Kierkegaard's phrase.[2]

Hypocrisy is not simply a contextual nicety that helps us understand what Wolves in the Throne Room are "about." Hypocrisy is also directly significant in the artworks that Wolves in the Throne Room produce. *Hypocrisis* is the Greek term for the fifth stage of rhetoric: delivery. I shall argue why this fact is profoundly significant for understanding the powerful novelty of Wolves in the Throne Room's contribution to Black Metal. In particular, delivery is the performative dimension of rhetoric, which I argue is a fully causal dimension. By playing with hypocrisy, Wolves in the Throne room are exploring causality—exploring, that is, directly tampering with it. I shall argue that in doing so Wolves in the Throne Room allow for the possibility of forms of speculative metaphysics that invite humans to think about the real, even as they are trapped on the "outside" of their skin, unable to inhabit their own flesh.

THE SMOKING POOL OF DEATH

Like all good names, the band name Wolves in the Throne Room evokes many things at once. There is a throne room, which is ruined and overrun by wolves. There is a throne room, in which wolves are the queens and kings. There is a throne room, in which wolves accompany humans, subservient and protective. There is a throne room, in which there are criminals who have been placed beyond the law: *homo lupus* as Giorgio Agamben has argued, humans who may be hunted and killed, but not sacrificed.[3] There is a throne room, in which there are *philosophers*: "wolf" is Bruno Latour's term for "philosopher."

Circling around the name, then, like a pack of wolves, is a pack of questions. The wolf pack as question: Who let them in? Did they arrive of their own accord? Where are we? More tellingly, *when* are we? Some legendary Norse past? The far human future? The near human future? If we are in the far human future, is this 100,000 years from now, when seven percent of global warming effects will still exist, slowly being absorbed by igneous rocks—rocks made of various kinds of *Metal*? Or perhaps this is a post-nuclear holocaust, up to 24,100 years from now, while plutonium is still deadly. The presence of wolves and the uncertainty about the time are part of one and the same syndrome: the eruption of a basic, searing anxiety.

Like a tangled thicket of thorns, the calligraphy of the band's logo cuts us, almost illegible, beautiful yet strange. The symmetry of the logo defeats the compulsion to read from left to right, "to make it mean something." The matted fibers of the *Two Hunters* sleeve evoke unseen things, unseeable things.[4] Writing is twisting itself into the fibers and filaments of trees: cryptic, encrypted—but not divorced from Nature, only an outgrowth of the same process.

The fibrous calligraphy is of a piece with the "nature" imagery on the cover of their album *Diadem of the 12 Stars*: gigantic waterfalls shrouded in mist, the rocks coated with trees.[5] Rightly, this album cover is wordless. Nature is saying something to us, something unspeakable. The image, which cannot be pronounced, evokes the silent functioning of things. It is a word that we can see but which is unspeakable. This is not Nature as a correlate of human imagination. This is the nonhuman in its most fully post-Romantic mode, a mode that I here call *the smoking pool of death*.

This is the sound of Wolves in the Throne Room. The opening moments of *Two Hunters*, which begins as the faint sounds of rural ambience, yet explodes into a horrifying, beautiful, horrifyingly beautiful sequence of chords that My Bloody Valentine would have killed to invent.[6] The opening moments of the latest album *Celestial Lineage* perform the same mystery, as if Wolves in the Throne Room are miners digging under the sonic worlds evoked by the shoegaze band Slowdive, to discover a huge, abandoned cave covered with crystals. In this sense, the sound itself is speculative and realist, tunneling beyond the depths of melancholy into darker, yet more beautiful, realities.

Why a pool of death? It is as if Wolves in the Throne Room allow us to see what the Wheel of Life paintings of Tibet also allow: that life is caught in the jaws of death. The quiet rural sounds are only the tip of a gigantic iceberg. The frail flickers of living are small ripples on the gigantic pool of death, a pool evoked in the fjord of sound that does not assault but rather descends upon us with welcome, lapidary intensity—majestic, uncompromising. How deep is the pool? Why are there wolves in the throne room? The question of existence resounds, the question about existence, *the question that is existence*. Not an innocent question. Or perhaps yes, a purely innocent question, the only innocent question, but innocent not in the sense of ignorance, but in the sense of *never having committed any harm*, any time, any place (Latin, *innocens*). The kind of innocence that William Blake talks about, a disturbing innocence, not naivety, but armed to the teeth, with nonviolence.

And as the song descends still further into the next song, "Vastness and Sorrow," we feel the sharpness of those teeth. The screaming breath of a voice not raised in anger but pitched to the frequency of the violence of existence, moving with the precise torque of suffering. The ruthless gentleness of a 1:1 scale map of the smoking pool of death.

Why is the pool smoking? Mist seems to be rising from it. The cold hissing of distorted guitar and cymbals evokes the way water vapor rises from a cold pool in a forest clearing, the way dry ice seems to float around the dark hulk of bass bins. There is one pool, one mist rising: not a group or collective of instruments, but a single instrument with several heads, heads of wolves, like the vicious, mournful Thing in John Carpenter's film, a Thing discovered by a Norwegian who runs to the Americans, trying to warn them about a wolf that is not a wolf.[7]

Why *the* smoking pool, and not a smoking pool? Simply because this is a real pool, that preexists me. To use the definite article is to use the most powerful first word in realist fiction. There are many examples but consider the first two words of Oscar Wilde's *The Picture of Dorian Gray*: "The studio . . . ." Which studio? Why this one, the one that is here already, before I started reading.[8] I find myself already in the pool. I wake up drowning in a fjord, which was always already there. What seemed like little rocks floating on the ocean surface turned out to be the tips of gigantic mountains descending into the smoking pool of death. A woman's voice sings to me as I sink deeper into the coldness, spelling out a ritual catharsis ("Cleansing"). It is clean in the darkness of the smoking pool of death. It is honest and uncompromising. An immensely disturbing peace floats there.

There is nothing to do but decide to live authentically at the edge of the smoking pool of death, now we have entered the still waters in the dreamtime of sound. And so, the final song on *Two Hunters* is a promise: "I Will Lay Down My Bones Among the Rocks and Roots." Rocks and roots—human or inhuman; living or dead; organic or inorganic? With perfect inevitability, the album fades into the kind of faint ambience with which it begins. Yet the end is the sound of meadow birds, the sweetness of a summer's day. Was the smoking pool of death just a dream? The beginning is the thick night of crickets and owls. What beckons us out of this darkness?

Thus the two Nature samples function very differently, yet with an underlying unity. The opening sound is the beginning of dying, the first glistening droplets of liquid exiting the life-form as the inside of the being turns inside-out to face the music. The closing sound is the ongoing relief of the end of dying, the coinciding of the essence of things with the way they appear, the end of the rift, as the smoking pool of death seems to evaporate into a Norwegian summer meadow.

Where are we? When are we? Are we in Washington state, where Wolves in the Throne Room live (the beginning)? Or are we in Norway, where Black Metal originated (the end)? We are the world, it seems, finally—not in the horrifying affirmation of a Michael Jackson, but honestly, in a being-towards-death.

THE AGE OF ASYMMETRY: LIFE-IN-DEATH ON EARTH

The term *Heavy Metal* evokes the toxic entities that humans have forged since a decisive moment in what geology now calls the *Anthropocene*: 1945, when a thin layer of radioactive materials was deposited in Earth's crust. The term *Black Metal* suggests an uncompromising dwelling with the poison and intensity of the nonhumans that now exist: plutonium, uranium, global warming. Wolves in the Throne room dwells upon the darkness of Metal, that most chthonic of things, refusing to even try to attain escape velocity into the high orbit of affirmative culture that shuns the Earth beneath. As Steven Shakespeare writes, "We are a long way from nature worship. If we are dealing with a religion here, it is more like a contamination, in which spirit goes to ground."[9]

Robert Oppenheimer witnessed the first exploding nuclear bomb and said: "I am become death, destroyer of worlds." He was quoting the *Bhagavad Gita*, a text whose reception in Europe and America marked the beginning of the end of Western imperial overreach, typified by Hegel's philosophy of religion.[10] The statement resonates with what is spoken in the chorus of *Antigone*:

> Many are the disturbing creatures on Earth,
> Yet none is more disturbing than Man.[11]

Yet, the horrified amazement at the human power to shape the earth and ocean is simultaneous with a realization of the depths of earth and ocean and all the life-forms that swim, crawl, creep and fly within the biosphere that they themselves create. They are all death, destroyer of worlds, in the very fact of living: oxygen is the first environmental cataclysm, along with vast deposits of iron in Earth's crust. Both oxygen and iron ore are bacterial waste. On this view, the world itself is the destroyer of worlds. Humans have entered an *Age of Asymmetry* in which towering knowledge, including the realization of infinite inner spaces of freedom and creativity (exemplified by the Kantian sublime), is equally matched by towering physicality. We have entered the gigantic fjord of the next moment of history, without even knowing it.

This is reflected in art. Consider Hegel's *Lectures on Aesthetics*. In these lectures, Hegel argues that there are three ages of art, corresponding to greater and greater human knowing. First the symbolic phase, in which physical things outstrip knowing; then the classical phase, a Goldilocks sweet spot in which things and knowing seem equally balanced for a fleeting moment; then the Romantic age in which knowing outstrips things. As a Romantic himself, Hegel thought that it would be vertiginous inner freedom from here on out.[12] He made a mistake: he thought his view was the final one, the snow capped summit of human history. He did not realize that, even on the flawed inner logic of his own argument (which this essay does not endorse), nonhuman things would rise again to tower equal to human knowing, yet not in a return to Goldilocks classicism. Instead, there would be a face-off between asymmetrical opponents: the nuclear bomb exploding while Oppenheimer looks on, horrified. Infinite inner space discovers infinite outer space, not just outside the Solar System, but in the very core of things. In addition, a new kind of irony has been born: not the playful vertigo of Romanticism, but the deer-in-the-headlights realization that we are caught in the thicket of things, trapped in a thorn bush, imprisoned in the tree Yggdrasil. It is indeed a monstrous return to the "primitive" symbolic age of indigenous cultures, even if you use the logic of Richard Dawkins or Sam Harris. Even Dawkins exists along with nuclear radiation, and the knowledge of it. The three ages of art return mutated in the Age of Asymmetry.[13] Wolves in the Throne Room, then, is a tip of the branching Yggdrasil of this new phase of human existence.

The Yggdrasil tree has, of course, always been there. This is not a new phase of existence at all. It is simply a moment at which, even if you are a mechanist materialist, even if you are a pure idealist, or even a solipsist, you still have to deal with your garbage can, and the knowledge of where the garbage goes, and the gigantic island of plastic bags rotating in the Atlantic Ocean like some mad god. This is the moment *after the end of the world*: when the story we have been telling ourselves, that we live in a foreground whose existence is set off against a background, finally makes no sense at all. When I can Google Earth the carp in my English mother's backyard pond, the world as a meaningful background "over there" has ceased to exist.

The deep geological fact of the Anthropocene arises simultaneously with a deep philosophical reflection on reality, as the Kantian circle of correlationism that restricted thinking to, at best, a kind of PR for "hard science" and "modern" social reality begins to shatter.[14] Humans are now faced with the fact of coexistence: the fact that existence is always already coexistence down to the hidden depths of its core. Even if I am the only being in the universe, supposing this were possible, I do not coincide with myself. The *I* that is writing this is different from the *me* about which the writing is written.

There is a deep rift in the universe, the rift between essence and appearance: deeper than the difference between a substance and its accidents, which from this point of view is only the difference between *two kinds of appearance*. If we think real things are like boring cupcakes, and aesthetic appearances are like candy sprinkles, then we cleave to the default ontology that has plagued humans—and, I want to argue, all life-forms on this planet—

since at least the days of Aristotle.

If we want to go any deeper than this, and the present ecological emergency demands that we do, we must traverse dreamscapes in which the slightest misplaced footfall could land us in Hell. Why? Because it is very difficult to cleave to the torque of suffering. It is like trying to place one's hand against a rapidly revolving blade wheel. If we fail to match the speed of the rotation, we will be destroyed. The slightest deviation from the negativity required for what I have called *dark ecology* could be very dangerous.[15]

In addition, we are entering a state in which the overwhelming reality of things is accompanied by overwhelming feelings of unreality, for the very same reasons. In this state, it is easy to slip into a protective cynicism, whose hard shell seems to shield us from the worst we know, but which in turn is brittle. If current social conditions persist through the misapplication of cynicism, all will be lost.

The cynic has already lost, in fact. This is because "against the hyperobject we are always in the wrong." Inside the gigantic object called *biosphere*, inside the gigantic system called *global warming*, all actions, all attitudes, all statements are "wrong": incomplete, ineffective at some point, weak in places, fragile. Everyone is reduced to hypocrisy. Even the cynic: being cynical is a form of hypocritical hypocrisy, now that we know we are inside a gigantic beast. The cynic secretly hopes: if she vomits disgustingly enough, maybe the world will change. The cynic is a hypocrite in denial about her hypocrisy. The hypocrite, on the other hand, embraces her failure fully to grasp, articulate, or respond to the situation in which she finds herself. This is why Wolves in the Throne Room describe themselves as hypocrites. They know too much, as people who discovered one another through Earth First! They cannot unknow what they know. They stand on the edge of the smoking pool of death, along with the rest of us. Standing there is the ultimate act of nonviolence, a quintessentially political act, but one that purists may find apolitical, or even antipolitical.

To protect herself against the knowledge that her shell is fragile, the cynic may develop a certain kind of nihilism. This is a drastic misreading of the smoking pool of death. This is a nightmare, but it is not "just" an illusion. It is not just a "manifest image."[16] The decisive moment in a horror movie is when the protagonist accepts that "this is really happening." If we know that it is an illusion, just a neurological blip, then *it isn't an illusion*. As Lacan argued, "What constitutes pretense is the fact that, in the end, you don't know whether it's pretense or not."[17] The reality of the smoking pool of death is not the reality of some pregiven ontic cupcake. Nor is the unreality of a pure conceptual construction. We are the smoking pool of death, yet when I reach out to touch it, I only touch this butterfly resting on a flower in the Norwegian meadow.

If we want to go any deeper in our social and philosophical journey, we must descend into the smoking pool of death. Wolves in the Throne room provide a kind of musical antihistamine that enables humans to not have an allergic reaction to working at the depth necessary for retracing our broken coexistence with all beings.

NOTES

[1] Bradley Smith, "Interview with Wolves in the Throne Room 2006," *Nocturnal Cult*, http://www.nocturnalcult.com/WITTRint.htm.

[2] Søren Kierkegaard, "The Edifiying in the Thought that Against God We Are Always in the Wrong," in *Either/Or: A Fragment of Life*, ed. Victor Emerita, trans. Alastair Hannay (London: Penguin, 1992), 595–609.

[3] Giorgio Agamben, *Homo Sacer: Sovereign Power and Bare Life*, trans. Daniel Heller-Roazen (Stanford: Stanford University Press, 1998).

[4] Wolves in the Throne Room, *Two Hunters* (Southern Lord, 2009).

[5] Wolves in the Throne Room, *Diadem of 12 Stars* (Vendlus Records, 2006).

[6] Wolves in the Throne Room, *Two Hunters*.

[7] John Carpenter, dir., *The Thing* (Universal Studios, 1982).

[8] Oscar Wilde, *The Picture of Dorian Gray* (London: Penguin, 2009), 5.

[9] Steven Shakespeare, "The Light that Illuminates Itself, the Dark that Soils Itself: Blackened Notes from Schelling's Underground," in *Hideous Gnosis: The Black Metal Theory Symposium 1*, ed. Nicola Masciandaro (London: CreateSpace, 2009), 16 [5–22].

[10] Georg Wilhelm Friedrich Hegel, *Lectures on the Philosophy of Religion*, ed. Peter C. Hodgson, trans. R.F. Brown, P.C. Hodgson, and J.M. Stewart, with the assistance of H.S. Harris (Berkeley: University of California Press, 1988).

[11] Sophocles, *Antigone*, ed. Martin D'Ooge (Boston: Ginn, 1888), 52.

[12] Georg Wilhelm Friedrich Hegel, *Hegel's Aesthetics: Lectures on Fine Art*, trans. T.M. Knox, 2 vols. (Oxford: The Clarendon Press, 2010), 1:243–244, 1:438, 2:994.

[13] Timothy Morton, "Art in the Age of Asymmetry: Hegel, Objects, Aesthetics," *Evental Aesthetics* 1.1 (2012): 121–138; http://eventalaesthetics.net/download/EA112012_121_142_Morton_HegelArtAgeof Asymmetry.pdf.

[14] See Quentin Meillassoux, *After Finitude: An Essay on the Necessity of Contingency*, trans. Ray Brassier (New York: Continuum, 2009), 5.

[15] Timothy Morton, *Ecology without Nature* (Cambridge: Harvard University Press, 2007), 142–143, 181–197.

[16] Wilfrid Sellars, "Philosophy and the Scientific Image of Man," in *Science, Perception and Reality* (London: Routledge and Kegan Paul, 1963), 1–40; Ray Brassier, *Nihil Unbound: Enlightenment and Extinction* (New York: Palgrave, 2007), 3–8.

[17] Jacques Lacan, *Le seminaire, Livre III: Les psychoses* (Paris: Editions de Seuil, 1981), 48.

Baptism or Death
Black Metal in Contemporary Art, Birth of a New Aesthetic Category

Elodie Lesourd

Oh, Satan! One and unique god of my soul, inspire thou in me something yet more, present further perversions to my smoking heart, and then shalt thou see how I shall plunge myself into them all![1]

Mrs. de Saint-Ange's prayer could be the one granted to the contemporary artists who consider Black Metal as an inspiriting light. Satan offered them the most extreme creative, deleterious, and (maybe) richest form. Acting as Odin's raven-informants Huginn and Muninn (whose names translate to "Thought" and "Memory"), artists dissect a system, explore the sometimes obscure mechanisms which govern an organization, and appropriate the esthetical potential of their target. Thanks to the displacement of the subject and a change of state, they deliver a new vision. But does it mean that, using this cultural artifact as a referent, Black Metal is not an accomplished art? Does it need to be baptized by art to exist? If both cultural fields, contemporary art and Black Metal (so-called high and low), seem to be opposing or conflicting, what enables or motivates their collision? Thus we could ask ourselves, how do artists use Black Metal as a structural and thematic foundation for their work? A visual analysis of the referent signs of this musical genre allows us to observe the principle of revelation brought by art. The act of recognition presupposes to know already; to see is to learn. This semiology actually reveals that Black

Metal makes the most of art to enlarge its field of influence. Art has the capacity to suggest more than it shows and, using hermeneutics, the sign can be exceeded. If many artists apply a phenomenological approach towards Black Metal, it seems that only a critical analysis would allow an exploitation of its hidden potential. If art attempts to capture the elusive, to express the inexpressible, then art as an exegesis could possibly be its best interpreter. Finally, if this musical phenomenon witnesses its propagation, what matters to artists is an ability to transform Black Metal into a new aesthetic category. It means leaving behind the state of heterotopia to become an ideal genre to which the artwork could aspire to. Black Metal responds to our need for ritual and, when it is denoted by art, it reaches infinity. Just as Olaf I, King of Norway (995–1000 CE), spread terror with his drastic choices, contemporary art offers the possibility to expand and to become a real *Gesamtkunstwerk*. This is not a religious baptism but rather a philosophical one. It is a total immersion into contemporary Thought.

REFERENTS AS A WAY OF EXPANSION

Contemporary art depends on a subject, even if the subject is reflexive. The approach can be autotelic, or not, but it is always a matter of denotation. With the arrival of the media, art turned its interest towards popular culture with a creative appetence. It critically consumes and burns to ashes everything surrounding it.

Rock music, through its immediacy and its propensity to create meaning, was prone only a couple of years after its birth to Ray Johnson's aesthetic experiences—*Oedipus (Elvis #1)* (1956). It is when Rock music evolved to Metal music, a musical genre that inherently expressed a strong awareness of its own existence, that the art scene decided to analyze, quote, and dissect the entire underground culture. Thanks to this citational postmodern logic, several artists have considered Black Metal as a potential subject. Whether Rimbaldian seers or foolhardy rebels, artists have arisen who are deeply committed to using the musical movement of Black Metal as the object of their quest. This perilous choice is relevant because they are the ones who know the essential wealth inherent to this corpus. Thanks to art and reflexive work, the Black Metal movement reaches further than other subgenres: an extraordinary deployment.

It is interesting to identify these knights who, through their efforts to conquer an unclear and deserted world, have formed a new kind of legion. On an almost sociological field, we could observe that the number of these artists has distinctly increased since 2005. Obviously we will not go into details to present all of them, specifically because, facing a tremendous task, some artists succeed their baptism of fire better than others. We can notice that Black Metal, considered in its second wave, is a Scandinavian product, built and conceived on European foundations. Although in the last twenty years Black Metal has inspired international contributions (including Colombian and Taiwanese bands), it is still, for the most part, exclusively Western. We can make the same remark concerning artists (even if the art market distorts this data in some way). Black Metal music was born in Norway. As we will see later on, it is naturally there that, inspired by the aesthetic of the movement, the first artistic attempts emerged. But it's at the extremes that the power of Black Metal is revealed. While the Australian artist Tony Garifalakis (born in 1964) observed the waves of Black Metal as an adult, the younger American artist Grant Willing (born in 1987) contemplates and draws upon a past that now takes the appearance of ruins. It emphasizes that two different generational perspectives upon the events are made possible and potentially equally interesting. Black Metal keeps on fascinating artists long after its main originating events.

Figure 1. Torbjørn Rødland, "In a Norwegian Landscape 16," 1994, c-print, 140 x 107cm. Image courtesy of Nils Stærk, Copenhagen.

Torbjørn Rødland, known for his realist and violent photographs, seems to be the first artist to have worked on Black Metal, or at least with a Black Metal sensitiveness. In 1993, he pictured himself as the personification of a young lonely romantic ephebe overwhelmed by a feeling of contradiction, torn between the call of nature and the modern world. This "quarrel between the old and the new world" would be the main reason for his psyche's disorder.[2] Rødland's photographic series *In a Norwegian Landscape* (1993-1995) shares many concerns and visual codes with most of the first Norwegian bands [Figure 1]. Actually, he and the musicians shared the same *kairos*. They were aware that something was about to happen at that place, and at that time. It was not contingency but necessity.

As Rødland exemplifies, contemporary artists interested in this culture usually come from the same generation of musicians whose work they reference. Without doing a hagiography, this essay identifies the protagonists in order to understand what encourages them to work on a vile matter. Mainly we need to point at the referents. For many people, art simply reveals a few superficial points inherent to Black Metal, whereas, in fact, some artists are inspired by the strategies and the iconology that exists beneath and beyond the music. Other viewers question Black Metal and drive it into a corner. Although artists' approaches are quite various, their artworks often analyze many of the same precise elements.

Let's specify firstly that, though it is essentially the second wave of Black Metal that is autopsied by artists, the roots of the genre in the so-called first wave are not forgotten. In 2006, the Bulgarian artist Georgi Tushev outlined a fragmented face of the band Venom in a deconstructive, eponymous painting. Despite how the painting's geometric framework nearly erases the subject, the image actually finds its strength from abstraction. Intellectualization through abstraction does not affect Black Metal but sublimates it. The artist Adam Sullivan also quotes Celtic Frost, a band from the first wave, as well as Joseph Kosuth as major influences in his work. By placing these influences on the same level, Sullivan suggests that there is porosity between Black Metal and contemporary art, and moreover that Black Metal as a "thought-object" could be taken seriously.[3] In his cut-ups and collages, such as *The Real Voice* (2009), he presents an uncluttered vision of the Black Metal movement in order to reach a toned-down core—thanks to the use of an incongruous color code for this musical genre and a reduction of signs.

The history of the second wave of Black Metal, the very one which brought Black Metal out of its god-forsaken cellar, is appropriated by artists as the most immediate and maybe the easiest sign emerging from the movement. Insofar as music is immaterial, and ineffable, artists may refer logically to concrete elements, historical facts for instance, to evoke Black Metal. The facts and history of the second wave were almost immediately turned into myth, and art (of course) participates in the construction of a Black Metal mythology. In 2005, Banks Violette took over the minimal aesthetic of a burnt edifice in his famous work *Untitled (Church)*, unveiling himself as narrator. He does not forget that the main thing for a plastic act is to transform simple anecdotes into substantial works. Based on the artwork of Burzum's *Aske* EP (Deathlike Silence Productions, 1993), Banks's reasoning demonstrates the potential contained within these Black Metal artistic mediums.

Similar to the subgenre's history and mythology, Black Metal logos, the identity and incarnation of a band often extracted from bands' album covers, are an inexhaustible source of creation (as much as for the one who creates it as for the one who receives it) and probably the first aesthetic sign coming closer to art sensitivity. The American Anthony Burdin, a modern figure of the cursed artist, gives a primary role to the first Burzum logo in his censored installation *Voodoo Room* at the 2004 Frieze Art Fair. The installation recreates his former garage where he used to rehearse as a youngster, and where the logo was painted across a wall-length mirror. Here, the installation site is transformed into a nostalgic votive altar. Artists can use logos as ready-mades or in a will of appropriation, but it is important to see beyond the sign itself and to analyze its graphic or semiologic potential. The logos are indexical, but they must also be reflexive.

Figure 2. Erik Smith, "The Ghost of James Lee Byars Calling—The Coming of War (Absu)," 2008, charcoal on black tissue paper, 70 x 50 cm. Image courtesy of the artist.

From the image to the message, the lyrics have to become an object to manipulate. They are the voice incarnated. Even if melody foregoes speech, the lyrics are the body of the music. When the music stops, words stay. Moreover, words may also be visual objects, and artists are very adept at playing with semantics. Considered as elements inherent to this music, sound, and content, they are logically in the grip of artists' creative will. The lyrics of Darkthrone, Emperor, Absu, or Bethlehem are the subject of a drawing series shown in Erik Smith's installation *The Ghost of James Lee Byars Calling* (2006-7) [Figure 2]. This very clever work is a confrontation between art and history through James Lee Byars' figure, "the artist-apostle devoted to the faith's paradoxes," and the history of popular culture through its darkest side.[4] In a strong symbolic game, we come across essential visual elements such as the pentagram. The use of words in an artwork is a first step to abstraction. Words themselves could be considered as geometrical forms, but charged with powerful meanings. In order to understand the uses of these (sometimes cabalistic) signs and to reveal what is hidden, it is central to appeal to a hermeneutic.

Artists chose to put some distances to music itself and decided to interfere with the figuration, the incarnation of music through images.

Figure 3. Per-Oskar Leu, video still from *Vox Clamantis in Deserto*, 2010, (Film photography by Petter Holmern Halvorsen). Image courtesy of the artist.

Corpse paint immediately appears as the main specificity that refers to the genre. Black Metal culture is very codified and obeys constituent precepts of its musical beginnings. The visual impact of the movement is unquestionable and many artists colonize its endemic features, exposing it to the risk of caricature. Out of the wealth of elements within Black Metal culture that generate meaning, the foremost referent is the corpse paint. Undeniable, indubitable, and concrete, this surface and ceremonial element attempts a discursive rebirth under the cover of art. Like a narrative façade, it is an opening to a more reflexive content. Clara Djian and Nicolas Leto, a French-Swiss duo, reconsider the menacing and monstrous appearance of this masked face in their *Angoisse* series (2009-2010) by using stencils to refine the sign. Indeed, the use of this tool, extracted from art and crafts and urban culture, and so unfamiliar to this musical genre, enables the two artists to explore the capacity of this emblematic element, which could be reproducible ad infinitum. However, it is interesting also to allude to the activist use of spray paint by some bands at that time. The Norwegian artist Per-Oskar Leu uses corpse paint pertinently by shifting the subject from sign to incarnation, exteriority to interiority. In his video *Vox Clamantis In Deserto* (2010), he takes advantage of corpse paint to broaden its semantic construction [Figure 3]. He makes himself up as a grotesque Black Metal musician and emphatically performs again *I Pagliacci*, an opera by Ruggero Leoncavallo, in places historically linked to the movement (the Helvete basement, the Holmenkollen church). This strong work questions, not without irony, the notion of authenticity and transgression.

Revealing the man under the make-up does not mean humanizing Black Metal musicians. Artists, portraying these latter, seem to be turning characters into icons. Indeed, if corpse paint redefines the face, portraiture is often at the heart of an artistic work. In some artworks, the teenager is chosen as the absolute melancholic figure with infinite potential, but more often, as exemplified within the prolific work of Steven Shearer (who presents a real Metal Areopagus), it is the musicians themselves who are portrayed— *Longhairs 19* (2004), *Smoke* (2005), and *Davos* (2007). Thus Frost, Abbath, Infernus, Varg Vikernes, Gaahl, Beherit, Euronymous, Necrobutcher, and Hellbutcher have become real icons, in the original sense of the word. Yet these portraits of musicians have followed the opposite direction of genuine icons: Art transformed icons (objects of devotion) to "simple" objects of aesthetic delightfulness, whereas Black Metal musicians (aesthetic quasi-objects, dressed and wearing make-up as statues) became icons through art—maybe, finally, like art recently did with masterpieces turned into irreligious icons. Fenriz and Dead, in particular, are the main muses of the genre, symbolizing both roughness and fragility. They are the most frequently quoted figures.

FROM SEMIOLOGY TO A WAY OF BEING

Thanks to art, Black Metal spreads and gains a considerable extension of its field of existence. Artists do not stick to its dark, morose, and contemplative aspect. Although the iconology empowering the exultation of violence, hyper-masculinity, and martiality does fascinate, our most valorous conquering knights try to decipher the monster by giving an interpretation of it.

They try to reach a spiritual level and, at the same time, go deeper under the surface of appearances. Their vision moves away from the signs and becomes interpretative. They have a notable recourse to Satanism, one of the fundaments of the spiritual dimension of Black Metal. This Dionysiac and libertarian call, exhilarating boundless musicians, is undoubtedly one of the driving forces of the creative process. Satanism, exploited and claimed by many bands, is the affirmation of paganism's return—"give us the gods of paganism" begged Sade—and is also an openly admitted resistance to Christianity.[5] Satan is a recurring figure in art history (reappearing in the 11th century, not to be ignored in the 12th century, and resurrected in the 19th century). Since the 1960s, he is an enlightened and liberating companion. The young Norwegian Sindre Foss Skancke, artist and curator of the exhibition *Do what thou wilt should be the key to the world* (the essential Crowleyan maxim from the Law of Thelema), attaches great importance to evil in his pictorial work. Art pieces such as *Bringer of light, the world is yours . . . Luciferion!* (2009) present a heavy and chaotic surface where mythology, alchemy, and occultism are shamelessly mixed. His very style evokes Black Metal graphic design, a universe whose mechanisms and mysteries he perfectly masters. The clumsy and fiendish Satanism lauded by many malevolent musicians is counter-balanced by a Promethean Satanism, highlighted by artists as the bringer of knowledge. This Luciferianism, in which Satan is an erudite character, a pure creative source (notably mentioned in some Darkthrone's lyrics) reminds us of Romantic ideals. Intellectuals, writers notably, introduced Luciferianism in 19th-century art. It makes sense that contemporary artists maintain it, and that Black Metal appears as the perfect vector. By mixing pagan and occult imagery, artists reveal the links between Scandinavian devil's music and Romanticism. The melancholic and dark, rambling development of the psyche allow a celebration of knowledge. Obviously, the veneration of nature, the fascination for the past's magnificence, the rejection of morality, the cult of the genius, and a kind of nationalism are typically Romantic concerns shared with Black Metal. If Romanticism is an absolute art, does Black Metal's involvement with Romanticism turn the genre into an absolute music? Actually, it gains this state through art. It becomes pure, speculative, and its metaphysical dimension makes it sacred. Artists who recognize this "Romantic agony" find the aesthetics of horror and terror as a source of pleasure, the splendor of the monstrous. They reinterpret this referent with codes particular to art history, because their first aim is to fulfill their roles as interpreters. Raising Black Metal to a spiritual level is not sufficient for some artists who claim its destruction is necessary for it to obtain resurrection. Varg Vikernes, as a worthy and perhaps unwitting heir to a long philosophical tradition, expresses this process: "If you wanna build something new, you have to destroy the old first."[6] Destruction is a process to engender creation. The analysis (at times extreme) of elements extracted from Black Metal leads to its death, but promises also a rich resurrection. We have to go through this to reveal the power of the subject. Artists are akin to berserkers, those fighters who are hidden under wolves' skin in Norse mythology. They appropriate Black Metal's strength from within its own skin. This skin itself is still a powerful and frightening signifier, but its power is activated only when it is worn. Some artists, in a conceptual approach, do not burden themselves with knowing anything about that wolf . . . such is the case with the American Jay Heikes who, in 2004, used bands' logos (such as Necromicon's or Behemoth's) for amazing works on paper. In these artworks, the logos become open windows to forest landscapes and emblematic lakes. He does not try to decipher those structures but captures their aesthetical strength. The text disappears and a truncated landscape appears, creating a new unity. The fact that Heikes has no particular attachment to his subject proves the authority of the sign.

A last form of detachment in relation to Black Metal immediacy is irony. This ironical approach, distant from the core, is not the least intriguing relationship between contemporary art and Black Metal. On the contrary, it is absolutely relevant and representative of how Black Metal is now judged and used by a part of the art scene. The Austrian Michael Gumhold kindly and humorously mistreats the caricatural image of the Black Metal musician. He links this representation to the image of a baseball player in his work *O.T (Kadavergehorsam)* (2006-08). The player dons corpse paint, like a ridiculous mask, and his bat is covered with spikes, like the Viking barbarian club weapon used as a banner by many musicians. These distinctive attributes are transformed into ironical referents. Gumhold's scathing humor turns to irony in the work of the American Russell Nachman. In his paintings the famous Teutonic make-up is applied to ordinary faces, just as if they were wearing buffoon or devil's masks. The dark side of the human condition interests Nachman. He reenacts the Divine Comedy and proves that Black Metal can be the metaphor of our society. His *Palimpsest* series are really a rewriting of Black Metal and religious histories, and his crude caricaturist style recalls illustrations from the genre's first fanzines. A demystifying irony, tinged with primitive enthusiasm, turns out to be a useful strategy. These latter artists have succeeded in following the movement's trend towards self-mockery. This ascetic practice—we attack ourselves—reveals a combative *jeu d'esprit* and shows some detachment. It allows Black Metal to exceed the nihilism in which it previously seemed captive.

Inevitably, these artists give a sarcastic and embezzled vision of the movement, forcing us to simultaneously question the notion of authenticity in Black Metal when approached by art, and of Black Metal itself. Some artists attempt to do a hermeneutic of Black Metal, to give an interpretation of its codes and symbols, in order to reveal what is hidden beyond its elusiveness. It is a syncretic phenomenon that calls for many referents to exist. Drawing from the real as much as from the imagination, Black Metal creates a new reality: a hyperreality which simulates something that does not really exist. Meanwhile, Black Metal extols the virtue of authenticity as its supreme value. Artists point towards this fake authenticity to reconsider the genre's fundamental basis, and they know that authenticity is not substantial to the object but is, rather, an effect produced by the gaze. The almost obsessive approach of the artist Bjarne Melgaard towards Black Metal reminds us of this ambiguous status, oscillating between reality and imagination. His compulsive, often formally violent, drawings are dug out from his confused mental universe and coexist with more symbolic works, such as *Untitled (Portrait of Varg Vikernes)* (2001), a piece showing a small, bronze-cast head hanging from a bonsai branch. Is this a pretense of Odin's sacrifice or unfulfilled death wish? Then, in a thirst for truth, he invited Frost to perform in the memorable *Kill me before I do it myself* (2001), in which brutal theatricality brushes dangerously with reality. Frost's participation enabled him to leave the simulacrum and participate with both Melgaard's performance, and Black Metal itself, to achieve a new and sudden impetus of pure authenticity. Maybe we could say that, following Nelson Goodman, representing Black Metal is not copying it, nor is it only interpreting it, but it is defining it. Thanks to art's movement beyond signs' limits, Black Metal reaches new level of intensity. Artists challenge the notion of authenticity, the nodal point of the movement. But how does this authenticity apply to artists themselves? Do they really share its beliefs? Black Metal is a domain of thought that can be either exploited or sublimated by art. Yet, Black Metal also fuels art; and art feeds it back. Is that a fair exchange? Can we only talk about exchange?

FROM UNION TO BIRTH

"The road of excess leads to the palace of wisdom," confessed William Blake.[7] It could define Black Metal's destiny. The wisdom it yearns for could be conquered by art. But what could characterize the union of Black Metal and contemporary art?

The union of art and Black Metal cannot be compared to the marriage of Heaven and Hell in a Manichean framework. Though the dualistic oppositions seem obvious—art (an elitist subject, which supposedly incarnates beauty, goodness, reason) versus Black Metal (a more populist genre, representing ugliness, badness, energy)—it is crucial to conceive the reversal of those values as a possible discourse. This is precisely what artists working on this musical theme suggest. The "aura" of the work is soiled and perverted, but its referent grants a revealed beauty. Art and Black Metal are not contradictory. Far from it. Their fusion enables each one to reach a culmination, an existential finality. Art makes the inscription of Black Metal into contemporary history possible and legitimizes it. If this movement seems sometimes blurry, as regards to the difficulty to discriminate between the fake and the genuine, it reaches, thanks to art, a new truth. It exacerbates and shares many aporia with contemporary art. Both appear as escapisms, forms of catharsis, desires to discard certain fears and feelings of pity. Art seems to be the most effective way for this musical genre to reach an ecstatic state. It clears the surplus and lightens the grey areas. It enables, above all, the possibility of annihilating the nihilistic enterprise by putting forward the will of life, of power, of light. The baptism that art suggests is like a revelation, a way to access transcendence. It is "this structuring operation holding together a mass of events in a single history."[8] If Black Metal needs art to be completely accomplished, the opposite seems also true.

Could art be a threat to Black Metal's integrity, and a nuisance to Black Metal's development and survival? Perhaps the way art analyzes everything might tend toward dispossession, toward fading. Is the multiplication of referents a threat leading to Black Metal's impoverishment? The baptism could turn then into a sacrifice. Baptism or death . . . caused by art. It seems necessary, even vital, to take this risk.

Maybe we need to give a new definition of the way art comprehends Black Metal. If Black Metal is generally well accepted as a modern vision of Romanticism, rereading history backwards, "against the grain," we may consider another speculation on its aesthetical projection: Black Metal is, conceptually and artistically, Baroque.

It is about identifying this entity as a category, as a movement, no longer musical, but autonomous and finalized. It has irregular, chaotic, and changeable aspects; it is the imperfect pearl of music. Its strength precisely lies in its strangeness. It is characterized by its excesses, hyperboles, and amplifications, as well as its will to escape from a frame, to surpass and transcend itself. Through the prism of art, Black Metal has become a metaphoric beyond Black Metal itself. It is a particular form of sensibility that can evolve to an ideal genre aimed at by the work of art. It is by the agency of art that this genre has to lead to a pure aesthetic form. It perfectly incarnates the aesthetic identity of our time and suggests, by the reversal of values, a real change of what constitutes beauty. It brings new codes of appreciation and it is the perfect emblem of the current expressiveness. Conclusively, it's fairly obvious that the clearest thought emerging from all the possible theoretical labeling attempts is that Black Metal could be defined as a new aesthetic category by itself. It is also definitively, and literally, a *Gesamtkunstwerk*.

The young, Norwegian artist Erik Tidemann, for instance, tends to create a total fusion between the two worlds, art and music, and suggests an initiation to this theory. He commits himself, heart and soul, to his art. In his videos, he often appears in the middle of shamanic acts, something between black mass and activist performance, wearing the face of a freshly dead deer. On the occasion of the Nidrosian Black Mass, a Black Metal festival in Trondheim in 2007, he immersed himself in his research subject with his installation *Kick out the Titans*. Here, video and drawings are joined with beheaded animals' faces and dislocated limbs and presented as stage set. The fact that he takes part in a context unfamiliar with contemporary art shows that he takes risks with the perception of his work. Finally, it is the art scene that sanctioned him by canceling the studio he was granted. This event demonstrates Black Metal's potential danger to art. It's a threat, visually and morally, to the public. To come back to the roots of *Gesamtkunstwerk*, we primarily need to talk of artists who are musicians, and vice-versa. To look at the possibility of defining Black Metal as a new influential categorical concept is to accept the greatness and the strength of its association with art, and to consider it as the possible birth of a total work of art. Art finds in music a natural extension of its expression.

Figure 4. Dimitris Foutris, "Black Tuda," 2006. (Performance with Em Kei, Poka-Yio, Apostolos Zervedvas, and Nethescerial at Ileana Tounta Gallery, May 14, 2006). Image courtesy of the artist.

Incidentally, many artists are also musicians and many musicians have an artistic background. The tendency towards exchanges between these practices can be observed in the field of Black Metal as well. Dimitris Foutris, like many artists, played in a band as a teenager. He nostalgically refers to his own direct involvement with the music by inviting the band Nethescerial to his *Black Tuda* performance in 2006 [Figure 4]. He and three others Greek artists, hidden under large hoods and dark albs, surrounded the band playing live. Did the artists metaphorically appear as the guardians of an occult knowledge or, conversely, did they stand for a threat?

Some artists have strongly pursued this double practice. Sindre Foss Skancke is probably the most interesting figure representing this interdisciplinary tendency. Because the activity of a studio artist is largely solitary, he has naturally pursued a personal accomplishment in his music and added to all the already existing one-man bands a new company, the band Utarm. His deep exploration of the subject, multidisciplinary approach, and sometimes collaborative practices as an artist/curator, are elements recalling a Wagnerian *Gesamtkunstwerk*. He is one of the first to invite a musician of Black Metal into a white cube, not for playing his own role but to exist as an artist. Daniel Vrangsinn, the bass player for the band Carpathian Forest, seems to be attracted to the freedom given by art and tries to expend his field of creation with music at its core. He exhibited his video *Phobia* in 2009 at the Kurant Art Gallery during the *Do what thou wilt should be the key to the world* show in Tromsø. *Phobia* is a global project, including various musical collaborations, that visually illustrates the different songs of the eponymous LP (Misantrof ANTIrecords, 2010). Finally, Thomas Gabriel Fischer (of Hellhammer and Celtic Frost) explores the endless wealth of artistic creation in an outsider practice with a more personal approach. He began in 2007, by creating a series of painted death masks cast from his own face and painted in unique ways. Now, he examines three-dimensionality, with scathing ready-mades—dildos embezzled and transformed into religious objects. It is interesting to note that the approach of these two musicians reinforces, and even validates, the works of the different artists quoted before. Moreover, aren't the latest musical attempts of a few contemporary clever bands the closest approach to this desire to elevate Black Metal to an upper level? The challenging concepts and principles to surpass oneself are shared by contemporary musicians and artists. Post-Black Metal musicians and artists work in concert for its ultimate advent.

The unsurpassable singularity of a phenomenon makes it an emblem, perhaps even a new system of thinking. Black Metal is beyond music. It exceeds its function of musical genre. It radiates with its sepulchral fire on every side of culture. Art can disperse the clouds that restrict the passing of its rays, and is among the best possibilities to reveal the hidden star. Black Metal is a suffering body that illustrates, in the same spring, all the human darkness as much as its vital impetus. It belongs to an indiscernible zone between a finished object and a future one. If it is finished, art would be its extension. To plan it into the future is announcing its return. If it is not finished, art is truly revealing it. If we consider this movement as an access to a certain worldview (*Weltanschauung*), inspired by Romanticism and Satanism, the desire for transgression (based on affirmation and refusal) seems to act like the utmost source of motivation. With its intrusion into the art world as a rite of passage, Black Metal, as a symbolic form, aspires to an extension, a considerable propagation, a (re)birth. Art takes on the exegete function to unveil "the logic of sensation" of this epiphenomenon becoming a full aesthetic genre.[9] The works of art dealing with Black Metal, using semiology to understand its mode of existence, seem to be the finished product, the ultimate and final stage of the Black Metal project itself. Furthermore, following Susan Sontag, who declares that "art is not only about something; it is something," we can consider that art is Black Metal.[10]

Figure 5. Elodie Lesourd, "Ornament and crime (Hvis Lyset Tar Oss)," 2011, cut band t-shirt, epoxy resin, variable dimensions. Image courtesy of the artist.

NOTES

[1] Marquis de Sade, "Dialogue the Fifth," in *Justine, Philosophy in the Bedroom & Other Writings,* trans. Richard Seaver & Austryn Wainhouse (New York City: Grove Press, 1965). Originally published in *La Philosophie dans le Boudoir* (Londres: Aux dépens de la Compagnie, 1795).

[2] Friedrich Nietzsche, "On Moods," in *Journal of Nietzsche Studies* 2 (1991): 5-11.

[3] Hannah Arendt, "Invisibility and Withdrawal," in *The Life of the Mind* (New York: Harcourt Brace, 1978).

[4] Klaus Ottmann, "Epiphanies de beauté et de connaissance, le monde de la vie de James Lee Byars," in *James Lee Byars, life, love and death* (Strasbourg: Les musées de Strasbourg, 2005).

[5] Marquis de Sade, "Dialogue the Fifth."

[6] *Until the Light Takes Us*, dirs. Aaron Aites and Audrey Ewell, DVD (New York City: Variance Films, 2009).

[7] William Blake, "Proverbs of Hell," in *The Marriage of Heaven and Hell* (London: William Blake, 1790).

[8] Paul Ricoeur, *Lectures II: La contrée des philosophes* (Paris: Seuil, 1992).

[9] Gilles Deleuze, *Francis Bacon: the Logic of Sensation*, trans. Daniel Smith (London: Continuum, 2003). Originally published as *Francis Bacon: logique de la sensation* (Paris: éditions de la Différence, 1981).

[10] Susan Sontag, "On Style," in *Against Interpretation and Other Essays* (New York: Farrar, Straus and Giroux, 1966).

The night is no longer dead;
it has a life of its own.

Alexander Binder
Gast Bouschet and Nadine Hilbert
Ibrahim R. Ineke
Alessandro Keegan
Irena Knezevic
Allen Linder
Gean Moreno
Nine Yamamoto-Masson

it has a life of its own.

There's the sign: the loud screech of the final sound-check bursts through the dark venue. And then an eerie silence. The muffled jabber of voices return to swim around my ankles once more, briefly, reminding me that others are here. I have enough time to weave through the fog, towards the front of the stage, and clear my mind with one, deep, resolutive exhale. . . . Wait for the sonic tide to break. And then, it hits. A deluge. A solid mass. First the long and deep waves of the bass tones. I close my eyes and fall. Struggling briefly to orientate myself. Shifting. I grasp out in an attempt to discover an analytical path towards understanding—What is happening to me?—before releasing this part of my mind that must find-a-way-through. It floods over me, through me: simultaneously enveloping and penetrating. I stand, stepping my feet apart—slightly—to align with my shoulders, firmly planted within this massive textual density that is spreading like layers of gauze, pervading the space. The vocals begin, emitting short waves, occasionally piercing out from underneath the lengths of the guitar and drums. I feel sonic pressure, released by the amplifier, pushing against my wrists and throat, and am overcome with the sensation of sounds swirling around me, immersing me, plummeting into my ears. Everything that was solid is now porous. I stand, exercising the strategic and exhilarating tightening and releasing of tension maintained throughout the set. Giving in to the sensation of being suspended, the pleasure of being lost, of not expecting, the impossible…

When Philip Tagg writes on the structure of Western music, in his *Introductory Notes to the Semiotics of Music,* melody (since the Renaissance) is described as a linear, sequential entity, standing in front of the texture of the accompaniment.[1] It is a recognizable voice, premiering high above the—sometimes indistinguishable—ambiance of the music. Typically (in occidental music) the vocalist leads, as the premier focal point of the performance, providing a single entry-point through lucid lyrics and chorus. With a profane gesture, Black Metal inverses this—counteracting structural hierarchy and its inherent monotheism. In describing the polyphonic, or polycentric, Tagg aptly cites the secular, visual compositions within paintings by Hieronymus Bosch or Pieter Bruegel the Elder. So many entry-points arise from the cacophonous moment of inception that there appear to be none-at-all. There is an all-at-once-ness to everything. Eyes and ears dart across obscured terrains and a yawning void expands. Perhaps, if there is not one clear answer, there are no answers? Nihilism is an exit strategy; you can always simply leave and let the vivacious sounds thrash against the thick doors that slam behind you. Or, you can enter it; let it engulf you. As if you were on the verge of drowning, you must enact here a mortal fight to maneuver through its elongated duration, affirming your own will to power, transcending your previously stagnant agency with a willingness to navigate through strange seas.

In the following pages, images by nine artists evoke Black Metal visually. The punctum here is obfuscation through texture. Within each image, complex layers imply both thickness and depth, offering extended spaces to be traversed, experiences to be undergone, exertions to be overcome. Traditional visual relationships between figure and ground are strategically reversed. Similar to the sonic event described above—where the melody is buried beneath a combination of the drum's blast-beat, the guitar's tremolo, and the amplifier feedback—each of these images emanate a dense, yet permeable, temporal and spatial confusion in their depiction of vast and immersive spaces. The perceptive viewer may recognize individual elements—trees, water, skies, stars, bones— but there is a rift: these images are not representing the objects that you know they are. Using demotic materials, they create a visual noise that is optically disorientating. It is a divisive technique. The mediations taking place are indeed the substance of the images: we do not look at these images, but *through* them.

The skeptical nature of encounter that I am recommending within this introduction (double fistedly: both sonically and visually) is a critique of the rational, analytical, representational, or measurable explorations of time and space, in favor of an experience that Eugène Minkowski recognizes within "dark space" or the phenomenological "lived space." To describe "me-here-now," you must abandon the notion of distance: the qualitative impulse to geometrically measure, and thus definitively distinguish, yourself outside and against your surroundings (and I would add, to equate your previous experience of objects: the that-then to the this-now). It is in this dark terrain that living unfolds and personal freedoms transpire. By intimately knowing and confronting this obscure and expansive depth laying before us we are able to actualize our potential and intuitively plunge ourselves into it. The simulated fog of the concert venue, the long drawn-out tones, the low rumbling of grays rolling across a photograph, multi-directional perspectives, simultaneity, the whirling storm clouds, our ability to reach out and wrinkle/ shove time and space, the seductiveness of closing one's eyes and navigating this private, seemingly ambient, space… it is all this, I feel, Minkowski perceives when he observes in *Lived Time*: "The night no longer is something dead; it has its own life."[2]

Within these curated pages, the obscure and abstract texture of Black Metal manifests as a veil that replicates the substantial darkness of the night's cloak. Night, momentarily displaced, perceived dead, emerges from this disjuncture, overcoming it with a raw vitality. Inversing figure and ground; interchanging melody and ambiance. The images express an opening of possibilities. Independent now from time and space, they seethe with the qualities of a transitional phenomenon and gain a life of their own.

-Amelia Ishmael

[1] Philip Tagg, *Introductory Notes to the Semiotics of Music* (Philip Tagg, July 1999). http://www.tagg.org
[2] Eugène Minkowski, *Lived Time*, trans.by Nancy Metzel (Northwestern University, 1970), 405.

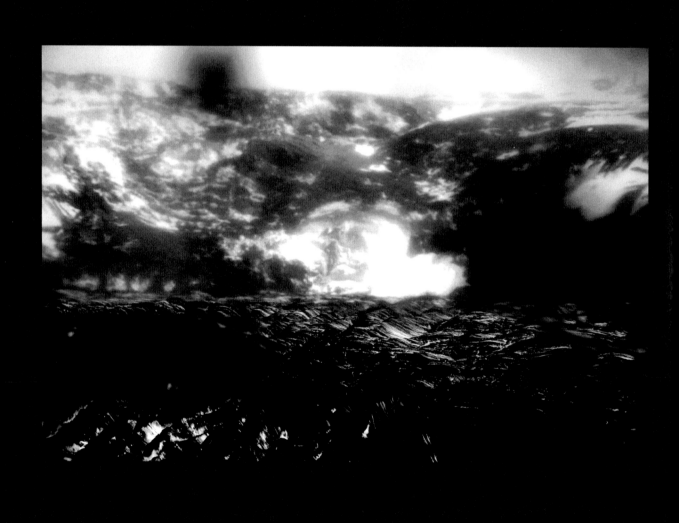

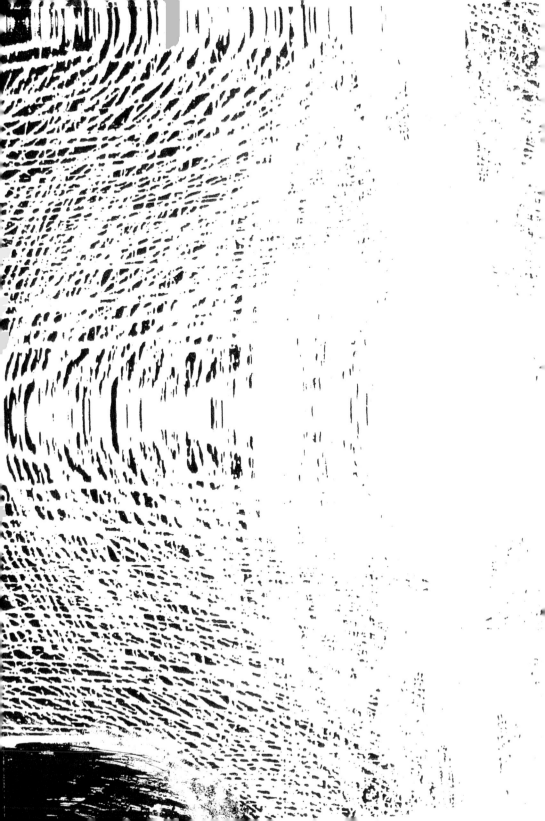

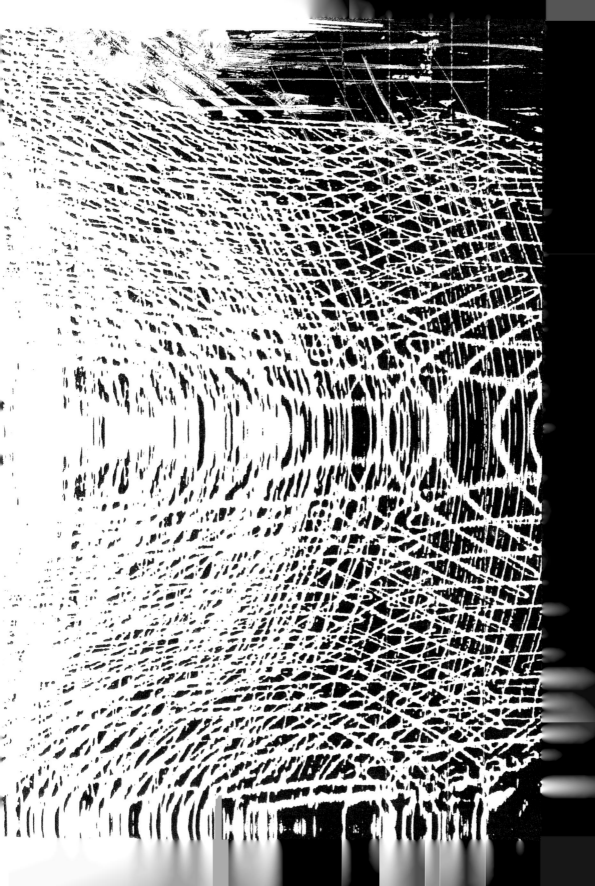

Alexander Binder

Pages 4-5: *Untitled (Traum)*, 2009
Page 14: *Untitled (Golgatha)*, 2011
Page 15: *Untitled (Golgatha)*, 2011

Alexander Binder was born on the Halloween night of 1976, in the Black Forest/Germany. He's a totally self-taught photographer, having never attended a photo class in his life. Even his lenses are mostly self-built from optical toys, old soviet cameras, prisms, or plastic crap. A fan of Hans Bellmer and Herbert List, Alexander creates mystical and ethereal photos that are characterized by a strong passion for the spiritual, the surreal, and the occult.
www.alexanderbinder.de

Gast Bouschet and Nadine Hilbert

Page 6: *Grímsvötn*, 2011
Page 7: *Grímsvötn*, 2011

On May 22, 2011, Iceland's most active volcano—Grímsvötn—erupted full force, sending a cloud of ash 15 kilometers in the air. The pictures here were taken in early June 2011, while a thick layer of dust and ash still covered parts of the Vatnajökull glacier. The partially blurred images are the result of experimental techniques, based on optical lens mistreatment by means of volcanic dust and ice as well as camera damage. Our work investigates the aesthetics and ethics of a threshold between inside and out, hiding and showing. It depicts the planet as a complex system and reflects man's foreignness in the world. We use visual handicaps to alter the visible and the ways of perceiving it. Obfuscation corrupts the process of perception and hinders the social construction of reality.
www.bouschet-hilbert.org

Ibrahim R. Ineke

Pages 18-19: Excerpt from "Blossom On a Thorn Bush" zine, xerografic print, 2011

Ibrahim R. Ineke is a draughtsman and curator, based in The Hague, Netherlands. He co-founded Baracca in 2005, as a means to "think out loud" his artistic praxis and to show work by artists whose approaches reflect or influence his own practice.

His artworks utilize and deconstruct the narrative strategies and visual structures of the comic book medium. Through sequences aesthetically influenced by drone music, they assert both the autonomy and interdependence of images in their use of layered xerographic noise, a slow gradual build, and hypnotic repetition.
www.melencolica.blogspot.com
www.spectralexistence.blogspot.com
www.baracca.nl

Alessandro Keegan

Page 20: *Untitled 2*, graphite on paper, 11 x 14 inches
Page 21: *Untitled 1*, graphite on paper, 11 x 14 inches

These black-and-white graphite drawings on paper share influences—such as nature, the sublime, growth, and decay—with the Black Metal genre.

The imagery suggests partially formed, primordial environments, emerging from light and shadow. In this way, they engage the theme of a beginning or a genesis. *Untitled 1* is a landscape scene with a shadowy grotto. The mountain-like protuberances in *Untitled 2* have a relationship to the mountain peaks often found in 19th-century Romantic paintings. I am interested in the subjective haze of Romanticism and fantasy art that is also a source of imagery adopted by the Black Metal aesthetic and other "dark" subcultures.

Irena Knezevic

Pages 22-23: *Failure of Visible Universe*, silkscreen on aluminum cinefoil, 2006

Failure of Visible Universe, conceived as an ongoing collaboration with the University of Chicago's Department of Astrophysics in 2006, is an annual index of vanished galaxies, imploded within imaging range of Earth's telescopes. The light that has vanished millions of years ago, has finally reached us— a record of good, old times. The scientific material in this work, based on spectral imaging, is used as an artistic alternative to the mathematic calculation of collateral damage. The astrophysicists involved are the guardians who watch time and space unfold without a flinch. Their powerlessness to intervene in the death of stars parallels, for me, the inability of consumers to intervene in the market forces and political decisions that affect us everyday. Especially pertinent in a time of recession and disaster, the editions were recently developed into personal one-offs where annual editions—corresponding to the year of worst personal failure by the person collecting the work—can be ordered. The edition is sent flat, to be crumpled by the collector and hidden away behind bookshelves, under beds, or any other place where it can gather dust and ruin.

www.allyouknowistrue.net

Allen Linder

Page 16: *Alone at nite in the forest with only a flashlight*, black ink on paper, 2009

Page 17: *Correggio's Buffalo*, black ink on paper, 2009

I approach making a drawing as an adventure. I begin with a simple mark, a doodle, a scribble. And then another and another. I make a conscious effort to try and avoid predictability. The mark making becomes a meditation which both focuses my vision and expands my peripheral vision. The marks build up into textured layers of density and complexity. I concentrate on the formal elements of line quality, light and dark, design and composition as the drawing continues to build itself. Forms begin to suggest themselves through the interplay of value. Some forms are refined, others merge and morph and others dissolve into darkness. I am attracted to deep, dark mysterious spaces. I avoid narrative reference as long as I can. I don't want to know where I am going. I want to be surprised when I get there. I turn the page upside-down and sideways, searching for content in the evolving form. All at once, I see exactly what it is and I assign the title.

www.lindersculpture.com

Gean Moreno

Page 12: *Untitled*, mixed media on existing paintings, 2007

Page 13: *Untitled*, mixed media on existing paintings, 2007

The images of this series are of accumulations over preexisting paintings by a well-known geometric abstractionist, which are themselves a remake of a project that he produced in the late 1970s. They have something to do with the possibility of the remake as it begins to crust and thicken and miss its grooves, allowing an Outside to geometric abstraction itself to start oozing in.

Nine Eglantine Yamamoto-Masson

Page 8: From "Ouvertures" series, digital c-print, 2009-2012, 8.3 x 11 inches

Page 9: From "Ouvertures" series, digital c-print, 2009-2012, 8.3 x 11 inches

Pages 10-11: From "Ouvertures" series, digital c-print, 2009-2012, 8.3 x 11 inches

Nine Eglantine Yamamoto-Masson is a Berlin-based, French-Japanese curator, artist, and PhD candidate at the Amsterdam School for Cultural Analysis (University of Amsterdam).

"Ouvertures" is an ongoing mosaic of photographs taken on the other side of suspended spaces. It plays with the lie within the aesthetics of the Sublime and lingers on the mundane that makes them possible. The enacted "ouvertures" refer both to the photographic apparatus as to the opening of an interstice within (or a disruption of) a habitus of representation and viewing. The present selection is comprised of images from Siberia, Iceland, and the Philippines.

www.kinemanippon.org

FROSTBITE ON MY FEET
REPRESENTATIONS OF WALKING IN BLACK METAL VISUAL CULTURE

David Prescott-Steed

INCIPIT/WALKING

Walking can be understood as a transitional practice whereby a person steps into, and through, a complex set of spatial and cognitive relationships. An example of such a theory of walking can be seen in the act of stepping through the doorway of a Gothic Cathedral (Notre Dame, for instance). Entering the westwork has long held physical and religious significance for Catholic devotees, symbolising one's departure from a world in which a conceived God is incomprehensible and indeterminable (a transcendental space) into a space of communion with that God (an immanental space). Each step into the vast and ornate interior space of the nave, and beyond, comprises a transitional ritual that puts the walker in dialogue with the sacred.

Consider also the Situationist International (SI)'s attempts to explore the many possibilities for interaction with city spaces through psychogeographic research (research questioning how the built environment influences how people think, act, and feel). Taking inspiration from the early modern *flâneur*, Guy Debord, Michel de Certeau, and other SI members would wander around Paris (and other cities) indulging their scopophilic fancies and treating the Parisian arrondisements as sites for creative, unstructured play. Privileging the "mobilized gaze," their *dérives* framed a negotiation with predominant, materialistic, and middle-class values.[1] In this example, walking embodies a transition through unfixed spatial subjectivities, within which the body could become "a veritable depot for departure and return."[2]

The significance of walking reaches beyond the kinesiological concerns of placing one foot in front of the other, of repeatedly shifting the weight of the body. Walking and thinking are intimately entwined. It is significant to a broader complex of cultural dynamics, but it often lacks recognition—like a quiet achiever who moves about under the radar. We can attribute this to walking's inherent repetition, for it is so commonplace in everyday life that it barely rates a mention; to contemplate every step would be exhausting and unnecessarily time consuming. Walking takes place, of course, but we forget about it in order to concentrate on other thoughts (e.g., of our destination and its associated tasks). Something as conceivably banal and monotonous as walking slips freely beneath the grounds of critical thought. In an abyss beneath cognisance—beyond illumination— walking endures.

In the context of Black Metal music's visual culture, walking might appear to be a rather irrelevant topic. Why? Black Metal is famous for its Neo-Baroque theatricality, allusions to Satanism and Paganism, corpse paint, images of burning churches, and death—things that present a challenge to the comforting familiarities of everyday life.

Listening to Black Metal music, we might imagine Odin waging wars, we do not imagine him taking a stroll down to the market. Walking seems to be too ordinary a part of the human condition—far too conventional to compete with Black Metal's provocative melodramas.

Truncated by the public's engagement with the spectacle of Black Metal, the less exotic practice of walking nonetheless remains an important practice within the genre. Its significance can be seen in two recent documentaries on Black Metal: Vice Broadcasting System (VBS)'s *True Norwegian Black Metal* and Aaron Aites and Audrey Ewell's *Until the Light Takes Us*.[3] In the first instance, Gaahl (the documentary's leading figure and the former frontman of Gorgoroth) insists that the film crew join him on a long trek into the Norwegian tundra. The hike draws our attention to the meaningfulness of the journey and speaks to the aura of solitude and endurance, of a confrontation with the unknown and human potential. Gaahl enforces: "I become what never fails, following the footsteps behind me." In *Until the Light Takes Us*, slow-motion footage of Darkthrone's Fenriz walking along a snowy forest path seems to evoke similar notions of the shadows of former selves seeking an obscured locus of self-authenticity. Both examples illustrate the capacity of walking to communicate a deeply planted Black Metal aesthetic. Thus, by way of walking—this atypical object of analysis—we find a new and unexpected entry point from which to explore the Black Metal landscape.

But there is more to it than this. Given that walking is a shared experience, we may capitalise on its commonality to consider how Black Metal might offer new meaning to our own (i.e., the listener's) walking. By using Black Metal to re-think an often taken-for-granted activity and to think critically about what is typically, uncritically, and automatically perceived, we have an opportunity to defamiliarise walking.[4] By defamiliarising walking, our attention may be drawn to its capacity as a creative practice that is culturally and personally meaningful. In this sense, Black Metal theory enables us to see walking in a new light or, for that matter, a new shade.

In order to delimit this turn in the discussion, I draw from a personal case study that articulates my own day-to-day experience of walking while listening to Black Metal music. Today, digital media fosters a curious tension between Black Metal walking and walking in everyday life. I have often found myself listening to Burzum's *Dunkelheit*, Gorgoroth's *Carving a Giant*, or Mayhem's *A Wise Birthgiver* while making my way down a bustling, city street in Melbourne, Australia and sensed a disjuncture, a rupture, between two divergent contexts: that of the unforgiving Nordic landscape that the songs, fuelled by Black Metal images, shape in my imagination, and my own material reality in a built environment punctuated by concrete pathways and pedestrian crossings. Both Tim Ingold's discussion of the difference "between walking on the ground, in the landscapes of 'real life,' and walking in the imagination, as in reading, writing, painting or listening to music" and Rey Chow's ideas on the Walkman offer theoretical context for the approach to Black Metal discussed in this essay.[5] In *Lines: A Brief History*, Ingold posits the act of walking as a kind of procession that finds him (at the outset of his book) linking walking to "weaving, observing, singing, storytelling, drawing and writing."[6] Ingold's "anthropology of the line" draws our attention to the line's capacities as a "thread" and "trace" that exists as multi-directional "transforms of one another" (2). He traces modern societies' notion that "straightness has come to epitomize not only rational thought and disputation but also the values of civility and moral rectitude" to the Renaissance, where it was adopted from the Euclidean geometry of more than two millennia before (Euclid posited the properly linear line "as a connection between points that has length but no breadth"). Ingold's personal search for lines in his everyday life found them "in exercise books, floorboards, brick walls and pavements." He explains how the idea of the line belies its complexity as a lived experience and that along which autobiography leaks, seeps, and bleeds (4).

> Alterity, we are told, is non-linear. The other side of this coin, however, is to assume that life is lived authentically on the spot, in places rather than along paths. Yet how could there be places, I wondered, if people did not come and go? Life on the spot surely cannot yield an experience of place, of being some*where*. To be a place, every somewhere must lie on one or several paths of movement to and from places elsewhere. Life is lived, I reasoned, along paths, not just in places, and paths are lines of a sort. It is along paths, too, that people grow into a knowledge of the world around them, and describe this world in the stories they tell. (2)

Beyond the positivism of modern analytical thought, and cognisant of the "doubt and confusion" (and reflexivity) of late modernity, Ingold notes that the "lines that once went straight to the point have become fragmented, and the task of life is once more to find a way through the cracks" (4). As a process throughout which a line is grown, such as when one writes or draws, walking is not simply a point-to-point interpretation of the world, or the division of the map of everyday life into points. Instead it can be understood as a means by which we might get "around" to a "place." Perhaps this will be regarded as a place of authenticity, reached in the course of a meandering that inscribes itself onto the surface of the world and upon the surface of the mind as a train/trail of thought. Ingold says that although "we are drawn to certain topics, and meander around them . . . by the time we reach them they seem to have disappeared—like a hill we climb that no longer looks like a hill once we have reached the top" (3).

Walking is also transitional in its capacity to transform how the body reads a space. But how might we make sense of that body? Remaining with Ingold for now, it is useful to outline the distinction he makes between "navigating" and "wayfaring" (16). The navigator traces a "complete representation of the territory" by way of which a journey may be "pre-planned." In contrast, the wayfarer's journey reconstructs, and thus reinscribes, the "itinerary as one goes along. Only upon reaching his destination, in this case, can the traveller truly be said to have found his way" (16). For wayfarers, journeying across a terrain (Ingold's examples are of Antiquity and the Middle Ages) entails reading

> a set of signposts, direction markers or stepping stones that enabled them to find their way within the landscape of memory. For this finding of the way—this guided, flowing movement from place to place—medieval readers had a special term, *ductus*. (92–93)

Ductus (from the Latin "leading") is used to denote the flow of the journey of reading and writing. This denotation can be reasonably extended to include the flow and open-endedness of walking as a transitional practice that takes process through material and cognitive space.

Ingold's way of relating "writing" to "walking" resonates with this essay as a space in which the flow of the former proceeds towards a view of the latter (and by the time I reach the end, what I expect to find might not be there at all). By sharing his search for lines in his everyday life, he uses his own experience as a valid source of data when seeking a way forward—and along the way, so shall I. Drawing from a personal case study helps to inform a nuanced understanding of the collision of Black Metal and walking in everyday life—what I playfully call "blackened walking"—in an experimental way that I hope will foster further discussion on this topic. As a Black Metal enthusiast living in a technologically advanced society—a very noisy culture—I often listen to Black Metal on my mp3 player while I walk. In this sense, Rey Chow's analysis of the cultural politics of portable music offers theoretical context for this part of the discussion with a flow on effect onto the others.

Chow's focus is not on Black Metal, but on Chinese Rock music. Nevertheless, given that "Chinese music raises many issues similar to those of rock and roll in the West," her insights lend themselves to Black Metal—one of Rock music's most extreme subgenres.[7] Particularly useful is Chow's reading of portable music, which reminds us, says Simon During, that "the power of the miniature is not only dependent on its cultural-political context. It belongs to technology and the body as well—here, to a particular conjunction between the two, enabled and made concrete by the Walkman" (462). Whereas Ingold offers a framework for thinking through walking as line-making in the built environment, Chow articulates "the equipment of modern nomadism" (474). She explains that portable music players support

> a composite mode of listening that involves multiple entries and exits, multiple turnings-on and turnings-off. If music is a kind of storage place for the emotions generated by cultural conflicts and struggles, then we can, with the new listening technology, talk about the production of such conflicts and struggles *on the human body* at the press of a button. In the age of the Walkman . . . the emotions have become portable. (474)

I am reminded of the SI's improvised meanderings, but just as much we may detect a relationship between Ingold's and Chow's insights. Chow's point that the portable music device "offers a means of self-production in an age when any emphasis on individualist positions amounts to a scandal" begs the question of whether listening to music, while walking, speaks closer to navigation or wayfaring (475). Are there conditions under which it might speak to both? We may note that "self-production" implies autonomy and lends itself to the DIY aesthetic, which Black Metal has long held in high esteem. It also sets up the act of walking as a physical and emotional re-inscription. In this performativity of the walking creative self, scope exists for the navigation of pre-tested and pre-planned components: the repeated song, the familiarity of streets. Wearing a band t-shirt might add to the "autism of the Walkman listener [that] irritates onlookers precisely because the onlookers find themselves reduced to the activity of looking alone" due to "hiddeness" of sound that headphones afford the listener (475–476). Autism, as a context of impaired social interaction, is here constructed by the listening body—the listener actively derives pleasure from the portable, mechanical apparatus. This apparatus (a structure of virtual files that is highly controllable: volume, time limits, custom equaliser settings) offers technological support for portable, structured emotions, and affords some degree of respite from the emotional proximity to the collective, the hustle and bustle of city chaos, that can overstimulate the senses. To walk is to imply a stand—"'I am not there, not where you collect me.' . . . a 'silent' sabotage of the technology of collectivization with its own instruments" (475). It is as if portable music is part of a coping strategy, whereby the listening body may embrace the soundscape of nomadicism in and throughout a highly rationalised public space such as a city or a suburb—the material reality under which the listener's body has been disciplined. Thus, we might imagine the contingent body listening to songs about the liberated body and following this Other (an alternative solution for living in the world) into the myth, and the mist, of the quest for the self. We come full circle, returning to SI thought in noticing that this sabotage without sound, but which is publicly announced visually, *détournes* the walking body as a means to enlivening its life-political powers.

TO WALK THE INFERNAL FIELDS[8]

> [W]e must recognise in the power of the imagination the creative impulse of life itself in continually bringing forth the forms we encounter, whether in art, through reading, writing or painting, or in nature, through walking in the landscape. (23)

Given that Black Metal theory is an attempt "to develop a theoretical framework on the basis of black metal itself,"[9] there is good reason to consider the prominent position that the role of walking occupies in the context of Black Metal visual culture. But what does thinking about walking mean for the music listener, i.e. the Black Metal fan who is also a part of this picture? It is a question that I have asked myself while walking down the city streets of Melbourne—a space geographical and climatically incongruent with many of the mental images evoked by the sounds in my headphones. To what extent does my use of Norwegian Black Metal music, as an artificial soundtrack for the material reality through which I walk, foster a kind of "blackened walking"? Can I speak of such a thing in Australia, a country in which mythologies of walking mostly entail long hikes through the bush beneath the searing summer heat? After all, it is not the threat of frostbite on my feet that I would face while walking through the Aussie bush, but ants' nests—not the headiness of altitude to contend with, but rather poisonous snakes and spiders.

Despite some assertions made within the Black Metal community against advanced capitalism, it is thanks to a technologically driven consumer culture that I am able to walk down a Melbourne street at 1am (or at any time, for that matter) listening to Mayhem's "A Wise Birthgiver" (*Ordo ad Chao*) on my mp3 player. Heading home after a (so-called) Black Metal gig in Melbourne, walking along the footpath at a pace fast enough to counteract the cold, the music reminds me of the scenes of Gaahl on the mountain or Fenriz's slowed down forest walk. I hear their conflicts with the modern world, but am grateful for the digital device this world has afforded me. Without my mp3 player, I could not carry the sound of trebly, fast-picked guitars with me wherever I go and bring to mind imagines of the shivering hands of musicians, playing and recording music in the icy tundra, as I step onto a tram or train during the morning commute.

These days, my experience of extreme music is much different than when I first became a fan. I remember being fifteen-years old—a time of emotional and intellectual transition, fuelled mostly by raging hormones—bored with Metallica and with Iron

Maiden's vibrantly coloured cover artwork. I remember returning home one day, sitting down on the beige lounge-room carpet of the family home, and playing Morbid Angel's *Alters of Madness* LP for the very first time. Not only because the sounds I heard diverged from what I had taken to be culturally acceptable, the music spoke to me about self-authenticity. What I heard was self-empowerment, a proxy voice for my own sense of self-creative potential, and my own dialogue with the past and with future possibilities. This kind of substitution is so common in music fandom that it verges on sociological cliché. Regardless, it has evolved two-fold: 1) in terms of the bands which have, like those before them, taken up high rotation on my music players, and 2) in terms of the music-playing technology itself becoming smaller, lighter, cheaper, and more portable.

Twenty years ago, I was listening to extreme music, learning the lyrics, and responding emotionally and intellectual to its various levels of creative content within the four walls of my parents' home. I knew nothing of capitalism or of how it continuously framed my everyday experience. Today, I am able to take Black Metal with me into the broader social sphere and, with it, a more informed understanding of my cultural surroundings. I can use it as a soundtrack to monotonous daily tasks—from doing the dishes to Trelldom (*Til Minne . . .*), to quick-stepping down an escalator in an underground train station with *Forces of Satan Storms* surging through my mind.[10] I am surely not the only one, for despite any allusions to individual empowerment that I might draw from this experience, it is, even if challenged by geography, one that is shared.

It is in these moments that I sense a rupture in time and space, a tension between mental images (the Norwegian landscape) and a material reality (a city environment) that informs the meaning I make of my actions. It is in this convergence that the blackening of walking becomes conceivable; portable music enables this experience. In "Listening Otherwise, Music Miniaturized: A Different Type of Question About Revolution," Rey Chow draws attention to the communicative and transformative power of the Walkman:

> We do not return to real individual or private emotions when we use the Walkman: rather the Walkman's artificiality makes us aware of the impending presence of the collective, which summons us with the infallibility of the sleepwalker. At the same time, what the Walkman provides is the possibility of a barrier, a blockage between 'me' and the world, so that, as in moments of undisturbed sleep, I can disappear as a listener playing music. The Walkman allows me, in other words, to be missing—to be a missing part of history, to which I say: "I am not there, not where you collect me." (475)

Chow tells me that by walking down the street listening to Gorgoroth (for example) I go "missing," figuratively speaking, by way of taking a cognitive retreat from the very collective that I physically move amongst. Chow is not speaking of any specific genre of music, but by considering the theory in relation to Black Metal, I am bringing to light a greater coincidence: the notion of "disappearance" and "missing" in history speaks to Black Metal's cultural conflict with a long-dominant Christian culture, and of the lengths to which the genre's "inner circles" have gone to negotiate this conflict. Portable music is said to foster a blockage between self and society and, in this withdrawal from conventional forces, it renders such a walker almost shadowlike. We may remember Rolston's insight regarding the necessity of distance for individualisation, and think of corpse paint as being uncannily illustrative.

But, if it is too dramatic to speak of the dead among the living (albeit in keeping with Black Metal theatricality), we can at least consider the way that a railroad switch moves rails laterally from one position to another; this blockage redirects the walker to a new spatial possibility and a renewed social relationship. Chow's use of the dream metaphor is also interesting, when thinking about the blackening of walking in everyday life, given the daydream's reputation for indulging the self in mind-wandering. But whether the landscape of the mind should be distinguished from the real world, and thus how we might understand their convergence, is an issue that Tim Ingold has investigated.

To summarise, Ingold asks about the difference "between walking on the ground, in the landscapes of 'real life', and walking in the imagination, as in reading, writing, painting or listening to music" (15). He discusses four examples: the monastic practices of early medieval Europe; the painting tradition of the Yolngu, an indigenous Australian people; the writings of Wassily Kandinsky; and a treatise by the 10th-century Chinese landscape painter Ching Hao. In each instance, Ingold finds appreciation for convergence between pictures in the mind and materiality—pointing to a significant overlap between "the terrains of the imagination and of 'real life'" (23). The medieval monastic practitioners, for instance, "regarded themselves as wayfarers, travelling in their minds from place to place, and composing their thoughts as they went along by drawing on, or 'pulling in,' ideas lodged in places previously visited." Reading through Hao's *Notes on Brush-work*, Ingold observes how

> the mental and the material, or the terrains of the imagination and the physical environment, run into one another to the extent of being barely distinguishable. They are like countries whose borders are thrown wide open to two-way traffic which, in passing from one country to the other, has to cross no ontological barrier. Such free passage is an offence to modern thought . . . . (17)

This is valuable for our purposes, given that modern thought (in view of Vikernes's,

Gaahl's, and Fenriz's comments) is an offence to the roots of Norwegian Black Metal. The mental images that the music evokes, its triggering of memories, may also be recognised as "outward, sensible forms that give shape to the inner generative impulse that is life itself."[11] As one such form, a shared worldly shape, walking is a vehicle for an existential impulse, sometimes also a motivating anxiety. The borderlessness of cognitive terrain and physical reality permit not the conflation, per se, but a kind of collaboration of one with the other. In terms of my own experience as a Black Metal listener, this has been the coupling of a conceivably empowered, assertive, and proactive body of thoughts and meanings with my own decision-making processes.

OF ICE AND MOVEMENT . . .[12]

There is something intriguing about the image of black-clad figures moving through a predominantly Lutheran, picture-postcard Norway. Peter Beste's photograph of Einar "Kvitrafn" Selvik, standing in a cobbled Bergen street, captures the moment when an elderly lady sees him, and his stare at the camera includes us in this tension. At the centre of this triangulation of space, bracketed by the human subjects, is distance itself. Kvitrafn's shirtless torso (covered only by his long, straight, blonde hair) is seen in profile while his face is turned leftward towards the camera. His posture implies that Beste's request to take a photograph might have interrupted Kvitrafn's passage through the village towards an unseen destination. The dynamism between the self and the culture that is expressed here reminds me of Holmes Rolston's idea that

> there is a relative solitude that is essential for personal integration—a separateness complementary to human community, its polar opposite. Nature does not define humans in order that they may be cultured, but neither can humans depend upon society to make us human. Each must finish himself. As an eminently political animal, man has the curious capacity to individualize personal worth. But distance is essential for this individualization. So, paradoxically, unless one can come by a lakeside such as this, and let physical distance loosen the hold of society upon him, he cannot find space and sanity within which to establish and maintain the boundaries of the self. Without such spaces there is no togetherness—merely fusion and homogeneity. Alone we cannot be human. Yet we cannot be human until we are alone.[13]

The necessity of solitude provides a doorway into the relationship between thinking and walking—one that we can step through to discuss representations of walking in Black Metal visual culture. It is here, at the lakeside (perhaps similar to the icy stream in

Espedal), that we might bump into Gaahl and, if we are a film crew, may agree to follow him up through the snow-blown mountains on a walk to remember.

In full costume, Gaahl comes across as a formidable *übermensch*, quite at home with distance from common folk. We only need to take a look at his corpse-painted face and bodily adornment in the video clip for Gorgoroth's "Carving a Giant" to sense the intensity of his stage character. But, it is in *True Norwegian Black Metal* that we see him walking and can gain an insight on the practice itself. From this, we may build thoughts around how this resilience might translate across time and space, digested by the senses of fans across the world, despite the potential disjuncture that exists between diverse cultural and geographical circumstances. We will walk through walking (as it is seen in this documentary), and like Nietzsche in the Schwarzwald, make some notes along the way.

The image of the solitary male trudging through a snowy forest, synonymous with Black Metal, connotes the individualist's journey, the solitary and contemplative passage through the extreme natural environment. Understandably, when the VBS film crew (including Peter Beste) arrives at Gaahl's home in Espedal, Norway they are somewhat nervous about what is going to happen. There is a fear of the unknown confronted, at some times more pressingly than others, by the extra efforts that isolation imposes on bodily functions. As the co-producer Rob Semmer explains:

> . . . no telephone, no nothing. . . . His brother was the only one who had plumbing in the house, and his brother lived about a mile up the road. So every time I needed to take a shit or anything, I had to walk, literally, in ankle high mud, because it had been raining for seventy-two days straight.[14]

Initially in this documentary, Gaahl talks about the importance of self-reliance, of following not a universal God but the "God within yourself, because that's the only true God."[15] The "footstep" metaphor gives focus to Gaahl's abstract thoughts, and we begin to detect the significance of walking even before witnessing that act itself; the representation of walking is already under construction and speaking the language of Black Metal. As Gaahl continues, commenting on the presence of God in nature and nature's growth, we see the first scenes of his back as the camera follows him walking forward through the forest.

The rushing rivers, the forest (dense with trees and mist), and a vast mountainous skyline repeatedly set the context for this adventure. Waiting for a break in the hazardous weather, the film crew spends three days with Gaahl, after which they agree to follow him to a place that he considered to hold great importance. However, they are unprepared and follow him, as co-producer Ivar Berglin recalls, "blindly into the wilderness. Only three of us had jackets, only two of us had boots, and none of us had any idea where he'd take us."[16] Gaahl explains the route they'll need to take, warning: "It's quite a long journey." "We'll see how long we make it," Berglin replies.[17] They set off from the valley towards a snow-capped mountain in the distance. They set off, ill-prepared in many ways; Semmer, for example, has only plastic bags tied around his feet to stop the water from getting beyond his shoes. Gorgoroth's "Sign of an Open Eye" provides a suitable soundtrack: "There is a god in man, and in nature."[18]

As the crew treks with Gaahl through the shrubbery, experiencing difficulty recognising the pathways that Gaahl had taken before his incarceration, his previous conversation continues as a voice-over. He explains that he has "no interest in getting a flock of sheep that's just following me . . . then I would be just as bad as society is, so fear is necessary to separate the ones that's [sic] willing to be led or the one who choose to lead himself."[19] It can be said that, by using fear to create distance between himself and others, Gaahl exposes his vulnerability. Still, seeing Gaahl ahead of the group, with their exhaustion becoming increasingly apparent, provides a more convincing visual cue. The shots of the white wilderness would be completely at home on any Black Metal album cover. The crew carve a track through the thick snow where, high up in the mountains, the air is thin. As we watch Semmer, he seems to be suffering the most and is losing his patience. Struggling to breathe, he stops walking and starts to panic. Semmer's reflection upon this experience is telling of what many perhaps expect of Black Metal and how an interesting cognitive space opens up when a figurehead of the genre challenges these expectations, just by walking, and how we might have formerly thought of the activity:

> And at this point I just, fucking, went into a panic, and I was just like, you know, this is fucking stupid. I don't know . . . you won't even really tell us where you're bringing us, or why you're bringing us, or what this is about. . . . At a point I was just like, I don't care what the fuck is at the top of the mountain, you know what I mean? . . . It makes no difference to me. We're gonna [sic] jeopardise this whole entire project for some stupid fucking nature walk. This is about heavy metal, you know? This is about a band. This isn't *Field and Stream* magazine.

Gaahl has led the film crew into the middle of nowhere—an arctic tundra—where even the film camera is threatening to fail. We are told that they have arrived at a home built long ago by Gaahl's grandparents, who had had no choice but to carry each piece of building material with them from the valley, past the tree line, to the mountain's top. To the unsuspecting, this insight is enough to evoke a mental image of Sisyphus—a king from Greek myth who was condemned by the Gods "to ceaselessly rolling a rock to the top of a mountain, whence the stone would fall back of its own weight."[20] However, such an image comes under false pretences, for Gaahl has since made clear that this was not the home of his grandparents after all, but rather a hunting cabin.[21] While the story makes for a powerful dialogue with time, this dialogue is misinformed. Nevertheless, even as the illusion disappears, Sisyphus remains. For, whatever the destination, whatever its meaning, the ardour of the journey exists and that is meaningful enough. As Camus says, "[t]he struggle itself toward the heights is enough to fill a man's heart."[22] The journey is filled with itself, not relying on life-transcending mythology for accessing a greater, more unique or authentic, sphere of meaning.

Gaahl's voice returns: "The superman, and the ideal, will always conquer, or always rise above no matter what. But you cannot put down your sword, because then, then you lose."[23] Again, the shared experience known as walking is cloaked in individualism. The journey is empowered with a grand rhetoric of transcendence—more than simply a sense of achievement, or satisfactory exhaustion that might follow one's small-stepping triumph over a challenging natural world. I am reminded of the oil painting *Der Wanderer über dem Nebelmeer (The Wanderer above the Sea of Fog)* (1818), by the German artist Caspar David Friedrich, where the solitary walker, having finally reached the summit of the tall mountain, peers out into the mist-filled distance of his homeland, engaged in a form of Kantian self-reflection in which the human condition is the object of deep contemplation.[24] The "physical" gives way to the "mythical," but remains a vital anchor.

Friedrich's painting has been used in the romantic depiction of Friedrich Nietzsche. Engaging with the outdoors, for Nietzsche, was a celebration of the gift of life. He would have liked to tend more often to his garden, if it hadn't been for his constant stomach problems often confining him to his home. Nevertheless, when the weather and his health permitted, it was Nietzsche the walker who worked in an aphoristic writing style, preferring to jot down short bursts of thought. Perhaps his revelations about the *übermensch* (the superman) occurred to him as his legs moved, as his blood increased the speed of its circulation, and as his brain released enough endorphins to increase his alertness, further fueling his train of thought: "Only those thoughts that come by walking have any value."[25]

Nietzsche was not alone in praising the practice of walking. The Greek philosopher Aristotle (382-322 BCE) made a habit of walking while giving lectures, and his disciples are known collectively as the Peripatetic School (from "peripatetic," meaning itinerant, traveling, wandering, nomadic, migrant). The Peripatetic School provides a precedent for Nietzsche as well as for Heidegger, whose solitary treks through Schwarzwald (the Black Forest, southeast Germany) were similar to Nietzsche's in the way that walking took place *for* thinking. Gaahl takes part in a philosophical and physical legacy dating back 2,000 years—well before Christianity established itself in Viking Norway, approximately one millennium ago.

In Gaahl's case, as the journey progresses, the benefit of a clearly visible pathway diminishes. It is a trail under erasure by the falling snow (echoing the transformation of forest paths during Gaahl's incarceration). The passage of time ensures some degree of corrosion—comparable to the way that centuries of human traffic have worn away the names of those entombed beneath the floor of Westminster Abbey in London (in particular, visitors can happen upon a nameless 9th-century slab worn smooth by countless passing footprints). On the Norwegian mountain, walking remains; the footsteps made by walking identify the path in retrospect when it comes time to finding one's own way back home.

This tension is present, I think, in the idiosyncratic and rather paradoxical proverb that Gaahl articulates elsewhere in the documentary: "I become what never fails, following the footsteps behind me."[26] The twist in the tail of this phrase disorientates, but in doing so it also manages to express a location, as if the spinning itself, though vertiginous, could not help but imply the proximity of an organising centre—one that offers, at least, a place on which to fall and rest. For what I think he means is that, especially when the passage of time has meant the erasure of a trail—like the German fairy tale "Hansel and Gretel," in which Hansel leaves a trail of breadcrumbs so that he and Gretel may find their way back home—the ability to see where you have come from is part of caring for the self. It plays into the idea that knowing (even *feeling*) history enriches one's experience of the present and the future. It marks a survival strategy, a sense of certainty, in the face of multiplicity. Such a dialogue with time is fed, only in part, by insecurity, an existential anxiety—of course, the trail left by Hansel was consumed by hungry birds. Gaahl, in presenting himself as being in communion with the natural landscape, works to pre-empt this kind of vulnerability. In fact, to the extent that the trek draws attention to the physical limitations of the film crew, Gaahl's apparent resilience, by contrast, consolidates itself within the greater spectacle.

Using music as a catalyst for change is one thing, and sharing the drive behind it is another. There is a stark difference between "talking the talk" and "walking the walk." At the top of the mountain, in the thin atmospheres of the vast and seemingly uninhabitable tundra, with far fewer words than steps, Gaahl is nevertheless in dialogue with time by way of the persistence of nature. As Anthony Giddens (drawing from Janette Rainwater) writes, such a state of dialogue pertains to the autobiography as

a corrective intervention into the past, not merely a chronicle of elapsed events . . . Reconstruction of the past goes along with anticipation of the likely life trajectory of the future . . . a process of self-questioning about how the individual handles the time of her lifespan . . . Holding a dialogue with time means identifying stressful events (actual events in the past and possible ones to be faced in the future) and coming to terms with their implications.[27]

Gaahl's creative output seems to be an expression of his autobiography, framed by the Norwegian landscape: "Nature is a great influence for what Norwegian Black Metal is; it is . . . and that's probably the reason why it's created in these areas."[28] Of course "walking the talk" necessitates taking the listener/viewer/interviewer beyond the easily accessible facade of Black Metal's theatricality, and into its day-to-day social behaviour. It is here that we encounter the past of an other, unknown, almost anachronistic—but, all the same, intrinsic—emotional and intellectual process.

At the end of the *True Norwegian Black Metal* documentary, one of the interviewers asks a question concerning whether Gaahl felt lonely, and what it was like to be a lone wolf. Gaahl responds by accusing the interviewer of asking the wrong questions, of "not focussing on what's being told." He then commences a blank stare that lasts over two-and-a-half minutes. At first this response seemed rather dissociative to me, and I began to wonder where Gaahl's mind had wandered. Was it back into the forest, where the river flows between the trees? Was Gaahl somehow drawing strength, or sanctuary, from the essential solitude of which Rolston spoke—that separateness—as a way of indulging his complementarity, and simultaneously oppositional, relationship to human community? Was he exploring the kind of distance that is essential for the individualisation of personal worth? Having watched these silent minutes over and over again, I believe that Gaahl remains fully cognisant. Occasional signs of recognition in his eyes suggest that he's making the most out of a captive audience, keeping full attention upon himself. There is a sense of distance here too, but this seems to have less to do with seeking emancipation from others than in manipulating them, wherein proximity is vital.

It seems that Gaahl's invitation to take us for a walk into nature was always going to be the kind of reflexive walk that would inevitably led back to Gaahl and his relationship to the world. He points us in the direction of ideas and places that are beyond walking but, all the same, walking provides something of a carrier, a visual vehicle, for our exploration of these things.[29] It provides us with a material reference point by which to explore a space of Black Metal thinking.

EN ÅS I DYPE SKOGEN (A HILL IN DEEP FOREST)[30]

There is reason to suggest that what we are being shown, though manifest as the act of walking, is the telos of self-authenticity, where the goal affords orientation to a single individual amid multiple and potentially conflicting alternative positions. In the late modern era, the challenge of multiplicity is often experienced visually: optic nerves are overstimulated with different versions of similar prompts to buy more, consume more, and to believe that this will lead to happiness. The push to measure self-worth through consumer goods comes at a cost—something that is evident in *Until the Light Takes Us*. In this documentary, the subject of modern consumer society is one of which Varg Vikernes says:

> It's very hard to recognize the truth when you are bombarded by lies all the time, every minute of the day. You have to go to sleep, and even in the sleep, because you dream of the impressions you have during the day. You know, you're bombarded by commercials and completely senseless information every single day. If you turn on the TV, you're bombarded; if you turn your head in some direction you see some sign, some commercial, read magazines, newspapers, senseless information. The news are themselves products being sold. Everything is meaningless. . . . The truth is of course to be found, but in a sea of lies its just impossible to find it unless you know how to look, where to look, and when to look, and, of course, it's not possible to just get up in the morning and say "Okay. I'm going to find the truth this day," and go find it. You have to try and fail, and eventually you will weed out all the lies and you end up with something at least similar to the truth.[31]

Vikernes's point here denotes a quest for personal meaning, and it is conceptually tied to Baudrillard's notion of hyper-reality—a cultural condition driven by mass reproduction where the proliferation of advertising imagery seems to have been emptied of all its meaning (de-symbolised, like when a single word is repeated over and over again). For someone who is overwhelmed by the relentless circulation of commercials and their complicit ideas, the search for meaning can become increasingly urgent. As Giddens points out,

> [p]ersonal meaningless—the feeling that life has nothing worthwhile to offer— becomes a fundamental psychic problem in circumstances of late modernity. We should understand this phenomenon in terms of a repression of moral questions which day-to-day life poses, but which are denied answers.[32]

The dialogue with time is not simply about nostalgia for what has gone, but a blatant awareness that time is now running out, and a subsequent urgency to achieve some sense of resolution. As time marches on, the need, the responsibility, to make life meaningful is a matter of ongoing revision and renewal. It is a reflexive project that, via a critical engagement with society's norms and expectations, "generates programmes of actualisation and mastery . . . [but] they lack moral meaning. 'Authenticity' becomes both a pre-eminent value and a framework for self-actualisation, but represents a morally stunted process."[33] It is interesting then, in Vikernes's subsequent words, that he uses a walking metaphor as a means to structure a self-affirming thought:

> The truth is hidden on the grass, under some rocks, in a hidden trail, a forgotten trail in the forest and when you try to find the trail you will stumble. You will get some branches in your face. You'll make mistakes before you finally find it.[34]

Here, once again, walking is invested with the import of a critical cultural practice.

In Vikernes's terms, this practice seems to use the notion of walking as a means to forging a pathway through self-awareness. He views truth as having been hidden from sight, behind or beyond the clutter of modern life, presumably by the socialising agencies of Norway's long-established Christian culture. Given that figurative language in general is a function of abstract thinking in everyday use, this choice of metaphor is interesting in the context of Vikernes's incarceration in a maximum security prison in Trondheim, Norway. During this time, his incarceration imposed a clear and immediate restriction to his ability to walk very far at all. With steel bars and surveillance cameras demarking Vikernes's physical space, his cognitive space was exercised; he had the chance to read books that he would not otherwise have had the time to digest. Is the truth of which he speaks protected by or hidden within this historical undergrowth? Whatever the answer may be, Vikernes's "imagined walking"—his anti-capitalist and anti-bourgeois thinking—works to clear a space in which he might find himself.

In *Until the Light Takes Us*, the act of walking also carries the theme of self-authenticity as it pertains to Gylve "Fenriz" Nagell. Very early on in this documentary, we see the back of Fenriz as he walks through an Oslo street at night. The scenery is in stark contrast to that which framed Gaahl in *True Norwegian Black Metal* but, once again, the viewer is in tow—following a Black Metal leader through the built environment. During this scene, Fenriz speaks of his own musical path and his consequential loss of contact with Vikernes's political path. The walking metaphor is already at work, focusing our cognisance of Black Metal history.

But, it is the footage of a black-clad Fenriz walking across snow and between trees (later seen in slow motion for special atmospheric effect) that gives the viewer a sense of identity and meaning that endures through time and space in the face of adversity. We don't actually see this particular footage of Fenriz until we are past the twenty-one minute mark, by which time the documentary's numerous interviews have established some headway into the early days of the Black Metal scene. By this point Olve "Abbath" Eikemo and Harald "Demonaz" Nœvdal from Immortal, Jan Axel "Hellhammer" Blomberg from Mayhem, and Vikernes have all shared memories from the period when Dead committed suicide. Transporting us back to the present, our attention is now on Fenriz, who can be seen alone making his way through the snow. We watch him first moving across the fixed-frame from left to right, and then the shot shifts to another fixed-frame where he walks in the direction of the viewer, watching his own footsteps. This footage of Fenriz walking marks a transitional point in the documentary narrative, and creates a visual bridge between memories of Dead and Vikernes's comments on the desire to destroy the Americanisation of his community. Of course, footage of walking, as a cinematic device, is not unique to Black Metal. Nevertheless, it is an important part of the construction and communication of a Black Metal historical narrative. For this reason, the representation of walking becomes intrinsic to how we consume that information.

Following these scenes of Fenriz's solitary walking through the snow, we are back on foot as we follow him through the streets of Oslo at night. We follow him in and out of a shop before arriving with him at a make-shift secondhand goods market. Here, he recounts buying an old tapedeck, for 50 Norwegian krone, to use for recording riffs and rehearsals: "Fucking sweet!"[35] We then see him standing in front of a white background, announcing: "I refuse to stand court-martialed for making this whole underground movement into a trend thing. If it's anyone, it's not us, but I guess most people would say that." The tension between walking, standing, and refusing to stand rounds off the first third of the documentary and focuses our path through the genre.

With the documentary's aim to communicate the historical, ideological, and aesthetic contexts of the Norwegian Black Metal scene, it is barely surprising that the narrative includes glimpses of a militaristic march through the streets, comprising men and boys in uniform carrying rifles and Norwegian flags, followed shortly after by women wearing traditional dress, walking together, and carrying candles. Although unidentified, this is most likely footage of Syttende Mai (Norwegian Constitution Day, May 17). The annual event expresses national identity and Norwegian heritage, and in this context it reinforces the tension articulated by Vikernes, Fenriz, and Ulver's Kristoffer "Garm" Rygg that exists between Norwegian and Christian cultures.

Walking *en masse* has long had political force. The *mobilized* community remains central to the visual presence of various movements as a way of giving voice to values, beliefs, and ideas. Human rights, women's liberation, and gay rights are among many cultural issues that have motivated walking in many cities around the world. In protest marches, such as the March on Washington on August 28, 1963 (organised by the American Civil Rights Movement in opposition to racially motivated employment discrimination in the defense sector) or the anti-war rallies that took place in over 600 towns and cities around the world (from Baghdad to Chicago, across the weekend of February 15-16, 2003) walking has become a signifier for community—and, by virtues of this, *personal*—empowerment. Oxfam Australia's Walk Against Want (a 40-year-old event that has raised over $10 million for long-term development work in 28 countries) aims to combat poverty and injustice. The National Walk for Values events (organised by the Sathya Sai Organization of Australia and Papua New Guinea took place on Saturday, April 12, 2008 in Brisbane, Sydney, Canberra, Melbourne, Adelaide, and Perth) aimed not to raise funds, but as a gesture of commitment to Love, Peace, Truth, Right Conduct, and Non-violence. The Gay Pride parades that take place each year in cities around the world provide more examples of the power of walking as a communicative act. When made in view of a crowd, a tribute to Norwegian heritage can proceed as a festival—socialized. In contrast though, it would appear that Vikernes was more interested in creating a spectacle.

The Fantoft Stave Church arson, on June 6, 1992, was seen by many in the Black Metal community as a symbolic reclamation of pagan land that had been appropriated by Christian culture. It was intended, as Vikernes says of the crime for which he would soon after be charged, "to give people a shock—to make them open their eyes."[36] Even in the context of Black Metal's controversial history—overshadowed by violent, counter-cultural activities—walking persists in a way similar to how soldiers are said to be "marching off to war." Original newsreel footage taken in the aftermath of the Fantoft Stave Church arson re-used in *Until the Light Takes Us* includes a moment when a forensic detective crouches beside a gravestone, looking to be collecting a piece of evidence believed to have been left behind by the arsonist only a few hours before; it is a single shoeprint. For better or worse, the Fantoft fire was closely linked to the Black Metal community, and this connection is not contested here (I believe that its relationship to Satanism is clearly flawed, not its relationship to Black Metal). We do not witness the role of walking in this instance, but we do have the evidence.

In the final scenes of *Until the Light Takes Us*, directors Aaron Aites and Audrey Ewell return us to the scene of Fenriz walking through the snow between the trees, only now this footage is in slow motion. By showing us the act of walking in slow motion, we are invited to consider it in greater depth, to pay closer attention to this commonplace and thus often overlooked practice. Defamiliarization "makes things 'strange' to make them truly visible."[37] By slowing this activity down, we have the opportunity to see beyond its banal familiarity; the increased difficulty this editing choice makes to our observation invites us to consider it in a different way. What we find is the way that the act of walking provides a loose refrain for the Black Metal narrative. We are not just looking at walking, of course—the many details, sounds, and other images included in both of the documentaries I've discussed all contribute to the overall representation—but what we have for Black Metal visual culture, in terms of walking in particular, is something like a path of concentration around which that greater story is woven. It is a powerful cinematic device, for sure. While it is not exclusive to these films, this does not mean it's any less vital in getting a message across.

ACROSS THE VACUUM[38]

Given my attention to the philosophical and material interactions of thinking and walking, entailing readings of two documentary films, it is fitting to take into account Astra Taylor's documentary film *Examined Life: Excursions with Contemporary Thinkers* when formulating some conclusive remarks.[39] This documentary (also available as a book) comprises eight dialogues, in each of which one of eight philosophers brings philosophical ideas to the streets of everyday life. The last dialogue, a conversation between Judith Butler and her friend Sunaura Taylor, takes place during a stroll through San Francisco's Mission District. Here, Butler asks what happens when a person walks in the world—the role that its capacities might play in how we feel in, and respond to, our environment. What it means for an able-bodied person will differ from what it means for Taylor, a woman born with arthrogryposis, who cannot walk but continues, as do her friends, she says, to use the word "walk" when communicating that she is about to go and do this activity—hardly surprising given that the word "walk" comes from the Old English word *wealcan* (which means "to roll").[40]

I was also struck by the resonance between the conservation between Butler and Taylor, and Ingold's aforementioned distinction between the navigator and the wayfarer. Taylor credits an increase in the public presence of disabled people to the public sphere's increased accessibility: "people have learned how to interact with them [disabled people] and are used to them in a certain way and, so, the physical access actually leads to a social access and acceptance." Butler responds, "It must be nice not to always have to be the pioneer; the very first one . . . having to explain: 'Yes I do,' you know, speak and think and talk and move . . ."[41] She implies the relief of the navigator who, with access to established pathways, is saved from the physical and emotional hardships required of the wayfarer.

If walking entails posture, self-expression, and choice—all potentially as part of a stance—what might walking mean in the context of physical disability? After all, both Gaahl and Fenriz are clearly able-bodied. To see black-clad male figures maneuvering a wheelchair through the snow would say something very different; I imagine it would be a task of incredible difficulty, and perhaps bring them far closer to Sisyphus. Butler says that

> nobody takes a walk without there being a technique of walking. Nobody goes
> for a walk without there being something that supports that walk—outside of

ourselves. . . . and that maybe we have a false idea that the able-bodied person is somehow radically self-sufficient.[42]

For Taylor, the myth of self-sufficiency is evident when, because of her physical impairment, something so taken for granted in the modern world as walking into a coffee shop and buying a coffee becomes a platform for demonstrating personal ability and choice. Taylor says, "In a way it's a political protest for me to go in and order a coffee and demand help simply because, in my opinion, help is something that we all need."[43] By extension, Taylor's assertiveness is important as she enters the shop as a representative of disabled bodies and of how they are publicly perceived. There is a stark contrast between Taylor's mode of entering into capitalism as a disabled person demanding assistance and that of Gaahl and Fenriz (who, at least on the surface, both 'have' able bodies), who use their walking bodies as social resistance (my thoughts trace also, further back, to Peter Beste's photograph of Einar "Kvitrafn" Selvik in Bergen).

"What Can a Body Do?" Butler asks, flagging Gilles Deleuze's essay that, by the very nature of this question, goes beyond the traditional approaches to the body that include the Cartesian mind/body split, questions of the ideal form, and so on. In Butler's view, the question of what a body can do serves to isolate "a set of capacities, a set of instrumentalities or actions, and we are, kind of, assemblages of those things," and moves us away from ideas about essences, or "shoulds," to those of the body. To demonstrate how walking stands as a signifier of other possibilities Butler recounts a male, of around 18 years, in Maine who walked "with a very distinct swish [of his hips]—a very feminine walk." On his way to school one day he was attacked by three of his classmates and thrown over a bridge, which killed him. She is right to ask how a person's gait could engender the drive in others to commit murder. "A walk can be a dangerous thing," she says, if this is what a body can do.

Not only does Butler's challenge to "essences" of the body unsettle any claim to its viability as a signifier for authenticity, her conversation with Taylor nurtures a greater sense of how privileged Gaahl's and Fenriz's solitary walks indeed are. With this we both arrive and return. We return to the original question of what might be meant by the term "blackened walking," but do so having arrived at the summit of Ingold's metaphorical hill, for while walking and thinking are still intimately entwined, walking now comes to mind as something quite peculiar—other than itself. At a distance, we can consider how the filmic representations of Gaahl and Fenriz, as key Black Metal productions, somehow contribute to the myth of the able body as a pre-requisite to life-political power, positing walking as the predominant catalyst for existential reward. If a concept of walking benefits from extending beyond a normalised body, so too must the meaningfulness of blackened ambulation take physical difference into account (in a way that might further problematise the visible that "irritates onlookers," in Chow's terms).

In this case, "blackened walking" is seen to be less about the activity of walking itself and more about the circumstances under which one can move through space—walking not just for the sake of exercise, pleasure, or getting to the shops on time. With the modern world (invested in trains, planes, and automobiles), the slow, simplicity of a walk (Walking? How pedestrian!) seems to have lost some of its value. However, walking is capable of bringing one's focus back to a fundamental question of what a body physically needs to do in order to transition through, and therefore *go on*, in the world. Perhaps mourning the forgetting of the existential significance of walking, "blackened walking" pays respects to walking as the chance to explore self-determination and a readiness for the unknown.

NOTES

All video stills throughout essay are screenshots from *Until the Light Takes Us*, dirs. Aaron Aites and Audrey Ewell, DVD (New York City: Variance Films, 2009). Images courtesy of Audrey Ewell ©2008–2009.

[1] Anne Friedberg, *Window Shopping: Cinema and the Postmodern* (Berkeley: University of California Press, 1993), 68.

[2] Anne Friedberg, *Window Shopping*, 110.

[3] *True Norwegian Black Metal*, prods. Peter Beste, Rob Semmer, Ivar Berglin, and Mike Washlesky, DVD (New York: VBS TV, 2007); *Until the Light Takes Us*, dirs. Aaron Aites and Audrey Ewell, DVD (New York City: Variance Films, 2009).

[4] Viktor Shklovsky coined the term "defamilarisation" [*ostranenie*] in his essay "Art as Device" (1917), using it as a literary device to distinguish between poetic and practical speech. In addressing the function of art, Shklovsky explained how defamiliarisation works against the "over-automatization" that fosters formulaic cultural activity. Viktor Shklovsky, "Art as Technique," in *Literary Theory: An Anthology*, eds. Julie Rivkin and Michael Ryan (Malden: Blackwell Publishing Ltd., 1998), 16.

[5] Tim Ingold, "Ways of mind-walking: reading, writing, painting," *Visual Studies* 25.1 (2010): 15–23.

[6] Tim Ingold, *Lines: A Brief History* (New York: Routledge, 2007), 1. Subsequent references to this text are made parenthetically, by page number.

[7] Rey Chow, "Listening Otherwise, Music Miniaturized: A Different Type of Question About Revolution," in *The Cultural Studies Reader*, 2nd edn., ed. Simon During (New York: Routledge, 1999), 465. Subsequent references to this text are made parenthetically, by page number.

[8] Darkthrone, *Under a Funeral Moon*, CD (Peaceville Records; Music for Nations, 1993).

[9] Tammy L. Castelein and Bram Ieven, "Review of *Hideous Gnosis: Black Metal Theory Symposium* 1, by Nicola Masciandaro, ed.," *Culture Machine*, August 2010 [Reviews]: 1 [1–6]; http://www.culturemachine.net/index.php/cm/article/viewFile/403/416.

[10] Gorgoroth, *Twilight of the Idols (In Conspiracy with Satan)*, CD (Nuclear Blast, 2003).

[11] Tim Ingold, "Ways of mind-walking: reading, writing, painting," in *Being Alive: Essays on Movement, Knowledge and Description* (London: Routledge, 2011), 198 [196–209].

[12] Gorgoroth, *Twilight of the Idols (In Conspiracy with Satan)*.

[13] Rolston Holmes III, *Philosophy Gone Wild* (Buffalo: Prometheus Books, 1989), 228.

[14] *True Norwegian Black Metal*.

[15] *True Norwegian Black Metal*.

[16] *True Norwegian Black Metal*.

[17] *True Norwegian Black Metal*.

[18] Gorgoroth, *True Norwegian Black Metal*, CD (Regain Records, 2006).

[19] *True Norwegian Black Metal*.

[20] Albert Camus, *The Myth of Sisyphus and other essays* (New York: Vintage, 1991), 119.

[21] "Trelldom/Gorgoroth interview–Gaahl 08/07," *Black Night Meditations – Underground Metal Radio*, WSCA 106.1 FM, podcast audio, July 4, 2008, http://bnm.podomatic.com/player/web/2008-07-04T23_11_10-07_00.

[22] Albert Camus, *The Myth of Sisyphus*, 123.

[23] *True Norwegian Black Metal*.

[24] Michael Edward Gorra, *The Bells in Their Silence* (Princeton, New Jersey: Princeton University Press, 2004), xi–xii.

[25] Friedrich Nietzsche, *The Twilight of the Idols and The Anti-Christ: or How to Philosophize with a Hammer*, ed. Michael Tanner, trans. R.J. Hollingdale (London: Penguin Books, 1990), 36.

[26] *True Norwegian Black Metal*.

[27] Anthony Giddens, *Modernity and Self-Identity: Self and Society in the Late Modern Age* (Stanford, California: Stanford University Press, 1991), 72–73.

[28] "Trelldom/Gorgoroth interview–Gaahl 08/07."

[29] The cover artwork of Trelldom's *Til Minne . . .* (2007), which features a photograph showing the band members walking up a snowy hill, also utilises this representational convention.

[30] Darkthrone, *Transylvanian Hunger*, CD (Peaceville Records, 1994).

[31] *Until the Light Takes Us*.

[32] Anthony Giddens, *Modernity and Self-Identity*, 9.

[33] Anthony Giddens, *Modernity and Self-Identity*, 9.

[34] *Until the Light Takes Us*.

[35] *Until the Light Takes Us*.

[36] *Until the Light Takes Us*.

[37] Patricia Waugh, *Literary Theory and Criticism: An Oxford Guide* (New York: Oxford University Press, 2007), 216.

[38] Darkthrone, *Ravishing Grimness*, CD (Moonfog Productions, 1999).

[39] *Examined Life: Excursions with Contemporary Thinkers*, dir. Astra Taylor (Canada: Sphinx Productions, 2008).

[40] *New Shorter Oxford English Dictionary 2*, ed. Lesley Brown (Oxford: Clarendon Press, 1993), 3613.

[41] *Examined Life: Excursions with Contemporary Thinkers*.

[42] *Examined Life: Excursions with Contemporary Thinkers*.

[43] *Examined Life: Excursions with Contemporary Thinkers*.

BLACK METAL MACHINE
THEORIZING INDUSTRIAL BLACK METAL

Daniel Lukes

Far from being a marginal Black Metal subgenre, Industrial Black Metal is central in bringing out Black Metal's often disavowed appropriation of machinic noise and its critique of machine society. Through its engagement with "becoming machine" logic and robot apocalypse, cybernetic, and cosmic science fictions, Industrial Black Metal reconfigures Black Metal's drive toward the inorganic inhuman as vehement critique of capitalist modernity and the industrial death state.

LIVING WITH VADER

Ryder Windham and Peter Vilmur's official Darth Vader guidebook *The Complete Vader* (2009) chuckles at some early merchandise misfires and mocks a 1978 collectable model kit Darth Vader Van by manufacturer MPC—which "could be pitted against a similar white 'hero' van in the 'drag race of the galaxy'"—describing it as "curiosity that managed to slip through Lucasfilm approvals."[1] Yet maybe the makers of that van were onto something. In 2011, Darth Vader is still being used to sell cars. The Volkswagen Passat 2012 commercial "The Force" features a young child in a Vader costume, who goes about a suburban family home trying to use "the force" to no avail. When the father returns home, the child rushes to the driveway to use the force on the car, which responds by flashing its headlights (stealthily activated by Dad's remote key). The child stumbles back in astonishment, the father raises his eyebrows to Mom, and the picture of the technologically-ensconced nuclear family is complete.

In the intervening thirty-three years, Vader has become a household deity, guarding the heavily invested and culturally sanctioned intersections of humanity, technology, and industrial commerce. As human/machine hybrid, Vader is a poster child for a narrative of necessary and ongoing symbiotic human/machine relations. The automobile is at the pinnacle of this hybridized way of life: its rear and front design anthropomorphically reproduces a human face, with its two headlight "eyes" and grill "mouth," just as Vader's shiny black metal mask and helmet mimic the car's protective carapace and hood, also a lethal weapon. Yet Vader is also an entity that embodies critical potentialities. Cédric Delsaux's recent photographic series "Dark Lens" (2004-2011) digitally introduces iconic Star Wars characters and machines into contemporary human, urban, and industrial landscapes, "locations that are the makeup of our modernity: parking lots, peripheral zones, wastelands, forgotten places" (the Millennium Falcon parked in a construction site in Dubai, stormtroopers under a motorway bridge, etc.).[2] In one photograph, Vader is viewed from behind, a lonely figure surveying the construction of a massive, illuminated multiplex against the night sky: in Vader's world, machinic construction and imperialist industrial expansion never end. The Death Star, itself permanently "under construction," is a flagship symbol of this endless outward reach.

The influence of Darth Vader and Star Wars on Metal music is manifold.[3] Rather than tracing those literal relations, Vader serves my purpose here as a conceptual crucible and starting point for discussing Industrial Black Metal (from hereon IBM: ironic acronym unintended but welcome). A hybrid encounter between Black Metal (BM) and Industrial musics, IBM blackens the machine, but also mechanizes, grounds, and gives a pulse to BM. IBM draws out and clarifies BM's critique of, and flight from, Western urban capitalism's contemporary industrial machine world, presenting an antithesis to BM's much-vaunted escape into the bucolic. IBM also foregrounds the struggle between vitalistic and mechanistic views of the world, with the latter swallowing the former. The distinction between the Freudian death drive, understood as a return to the inorganic (becoming mineral), and Deleuze and Guattari's politicization of said death drive and machinic conceptual framework, serve me to trace how a BM/IBM dialectic favors the mechanistic model, underscoring BM's ultimate godlessness. BM's grinding winds, frozen tundras, and glorifications of the mineral world are read by IBM through the prism of apocalyptic destruction, machine science fiction, and the annihilation of the human, to predicate a mechanistic paradigm of existence: the even darker side of BM's bucolic and Nordic anti-humanism. Finally, I observe how the genre of Cosmic Electronic BM constructs a black box for humanity, a digital epitaph transmitted through outer space.

EXTINCTION POSTHUMANISM

It is arguably the case, in academic discourses and speculative cultural productions alike, that within discussions of "posthumanism" and the "posthuman," biotechnological meanings occupy positions of conceptual dominance.[4] Biotechnological posthumanism (increasingly associated with "transhumanism" and the transhumanist movement, and often served by an aesthetic and conceptual framework spanning cyborg theory, eugenic dystopia, and mystical transcendence) denotes an improvement on the human, a form of truce with the machine world, a state of gradual and inevitable symbiotic co-existence with machines, a panoply of human, machine, and animal reconfigurations. Slavoj Žižek interprets the Deleuzian "becoming-machine" as not a substitution of humans by machines (which is the *Terminator* scenario—"the old boring topic of 'machines replacing humans'"), but rather as a form of metamorphosis by which the human gradually incorporates machinic prostheses on the level of the body (pacemaker, hearing aid, surgical nanobots) and of the mental apparatuses through which we negotiate the social or the sociomachine (the *Matrix* scenario).[5]

Another type of posthumanism, which engages the arguably more literal meaning of "post" as in "after" the human (has gone), may also be identified. The field of extinction posthumanism channels various intersecting literary, philosophical, and critical discourses: the Romantic genre of ruinography, the "dying Earth" genre and apocalyptic science fiction literature, and eco-critical works on postindustrial land and cityscapes. It extends Romantic ideas of extinction and merges them with ecological and speculative writings of a world after humanity. Unlike biotechnological posthumanism—which imagines a humanity that lives on, albeit in altered form—extinction posthumanism posits and speculates an end to humanity, often a total genocide of the human species. Furthermore, it radicalizes academic posthumanism's project of studying humanity through a decentering of the human and a transcendence of the anthropocentric prism, by imagining worlds beyond the extinction of the human and the erasure of the human from the planetary equation. In doing so it opens up a speculative aesthetic endowed with critical potential across the political spectrum.

In Romantic ruinography an onlooker—or "Looker-On"—surveys and ruminates on the ruins of bygone civilizations and empires.[6] Percy Bysshe Shelley's "Ozymandias" (1818) is arguably the most notorious of these Romantic texts, insisting upon "a teleology that dooms all of material life as we know it" by substituting the classical cyclical view of history with an apocalyptic "necessity of oblivion."[7] Dying Earth science fiction meanwhile posits an end of humanity due to a sun that has gone too cold (see Lord Byron's 1816 poem "Darkness") or too hot (H.P. Lovecraft's and Robert H. Barlow's *Till A' the Seas*, 1935), or as an effect of plagues or nuclear holocaust. Fantasies of the world as a ruin devoid of humans, according to Nick Yablon, may function as imaginative frameworks to render visible social or political phenomena that may be otherwise harder to parse, serving to "unmask the conceits of the present."[8] The work of Mike Davis, in particular *Dead Cities and Other Tales* (2002), utilizes the conceit of the "posthuman ruins" to trace urban histories: through the speculative image of the city as corpse, an autopsy of its life and genealogies may be constructed.[9]

A recent such work, which imagines a posthuman world in order to construct a critique of humanity's ecological impact, is Alan Weisman's "thought experiment" *The World Without Us* (2007). This book describes what would happen to Earth if there were a total and sudden departure of the human species, emphasizing the damage humanity has wrought. The gradual deconstruction of the human-made emerges as "nature" operates "its reclamation project" and regains its (rightfully) owned planet.[10] The world as a conceptual totality is broken down into its constituent parts: what comes across through representations of houses that rot and collapse, cities overgrown by vegetation, walls damaged and destroyed by water, and subway tunnels that flood with water are the mechanics of ecological materiality—a "dark ecology" in the words of Timothy Morton.[11] Homing in on the "impact of industrialist-capitalist civilization upon the environment" that will outlive us—non-biodegradable plastics, landfills, petrochemical plants and nuclear waste, and "carbon dioxide levels (which) would not return to 'pre-human levels' for a hundred thousand years"—this type of posthumanist extinction narrative retroactively configures the human (through its erasure) as an alien invader, a destructive parasite, or an illness to be defeated.[12] By imagining the world as better off without us, Weisman is able to fashion his eco-critique, within which the human takes the form of an erased antithesis, alienated by consciousness from matter and the blind mechanical workings of the material real. The human is an aberrative and destructive exception to the rule of a mechanical and un-self-aware "nature." To return the machine to functioning order, the virus of self-awareness embodied by the human requires elimination. At the point of departure of the human virus from the global body, "the world without us" permits itself "a huge biological sigh of relief."[13]

Extinction posthumanism constructs a speculative aesthetic and political scenario that rejects capitulations to the necessity of the human and its industrial accoutrements, as if only through imagining ourselves gone (we will be gone if we continue on this path) can we force awareness of our own pollutions onto ourselves. Yet, there are more radical and antihuman end-fantasies, ones that further reduce the human as ghostly gaze. Weisman's world blooms and bustles anew with flora and fauna: foliage and vegetation reclaim the space temporarily denied to them by concrete and steel, whilst animals (now free of the prisons imposed on them by humans) nest under bridges and atop skyscrapers. The organic world blossoms again. This is "soft" extinction posthumanism. "Hard" extinction posthumanism, by contrast, manifests itself not as becoming-animal or -vegetable, but by becoming-mineral. Sigmund Freud thus explains the death drive *(Todestrieb)* as a yearning to return to the prior state of the inorganic, before the separation between "animate" and "inanimate" matter occurred. In *Beyond the Pleasure Principle* (1920), through an appeal to various contemporary biological texts, Freud imagines the death drive as "the forces that seek to guide life towards death."[14] The death drive is understandable to Freud as a biological set of instructions inscribed within the organism; it is a function of the metabolism which is programmed for finitude. This process functions on micro and macro levels. On the former, each organism strives to return to the state of nonexistence which preceded its entry into life. On the latter, organic life as a whole configures itself within a chronological relationship to the inorganic. In the beginning, there was cosmic dust from which organic life emerged and to which it seeks to return: the function by which "most universal endeavor in all living matter to revert[s] to the quiescence *(Ruhe:* rest, quiet, peace, calm) of the inorganic world."[15]

Buzzing, droning, and shuffling recombinating organic life (or biomatter, with its corollary in the form of human consciousness) thus takes on the quality of noise, to which the inorganic cosmos appears not as primordial chaos but as harmony: calm, serene, and functional—the metaphysical music of the spheres *(musica universalis).* Freud's death drive yearns for the exactitude of scientific intelligibility, where existential doubt and skepticism (endemic to self-conscious humanity) is replaced by a state untroubled by anything beyond the mere execution of its own inexorable and objective physical laws.[16]

Swiss band Samael capture such sentiments on their 1996 album *Passage*—which takes the industrial stylings experimented with on their *Ceremony Of Opposites* (1994), ratchets up the keyboards, slows the pace to martial rhythms reminiscent of Laibach, and produces a pristine and grandiose tribute to the movements of space, rhapsodized with glory in "Jupiterian Vibe," "Shining Kingdom," "Moonskin," and "Born Under Saturn." In *Passage* (passage between human and mineral?), the self is lost in the grand movement of the planets, as Vorph's dictatorial vocals enunciate lyrics as though they are unalterable laws of physics. A purely keyboard version of *Passage* was released later by drummer/keyboardist Xytras, rarifying the album's impact even further.

BECOMING-MINERAL

Under the conceptual umbrella of "depressive thinking," Dominic Fox's *Cold World: The Aesthetics of Dejection and the Politics of Militant Dysphoria* (2009) discusses the "belated" BM of contemporary US act Xasthur (belated because it cannot help but look back with nostalgia at the golden age of BM). Fox posits that depictions of a cold, ashen, or desiccated world (such as in T.S. Eliot's *The Waste Land*, 1922) offer opportunities for radical political engagement: "[t]he cold world imposes itself as final, terminal, because it is the termination of a world, its metaphorical freezing or blackening."[17] The "peak oil" narrative (and its attending crises for example) awaken us through shock, shaking us to action through an imaginative deadening of the world. For Xasthur's "depressive thinking," "life and death are identical: the axioms of life are axioms of death. There is no *difference* between being alive and being dead, except that the living suffer."[18] In Xasthur, whose contribution to the BM canon occurs through "introversion" (a form of self-overcoming produced by reading BM through the paradigms of grunge and nu-metal, two genres highly focused on a depressed recording subject), the self is shaken into action through a contemplation of the end:

> [t]he cold world of black metal is a deliberate freezing of the world, fixing it within a terminal image, in order that its frost-bitten surface may be shattered by anonymous, inhuman forces rising from the depths of the self.[19]

This framework provides a reading of the dubious legacy of the Burzum model, in which BM becomes a pathetic attempt to rouse the dejected adolescent consciousness, alienated into the fantastic (the Dungeons & Dragons orcs that populate Burzum's lyrical panoramas) and then violent anti-social action in the real world (murder, arson, etc). But not all BM is depressed, or functions through depressive tropes. Immortal, for example, embody another model, which tends instead toward the sublime and the comedic rather than the tragic.[20] Immortal's obsessive vistas over frozen and scorched landscapes, cavernous and frost-covered panoramas, and whirring, inhospitable blizzards ("Unsilent Storms in the North Abyss," "The Sun No Longer Rises," "Frozen by Icewinds," *Battles In The North*, "Grim and Frostbitten Kingdoms," "Where Dark and Light Don't Differ," "In My Kingdom Cold," one could go on) offer a more radical relation to the inorganic, articulating not so much a measuring of the self *against* the sadness of life, but a sinking into and above the harshness of physical and geological extremity—a becoming-ice and -rock, a merging with the minerality of the world; or a becoming-demon, dwelling within the ice realm. For Immortal, nature is more than a prop for one basement-dweller's depressive consciousness.

They rather embody a transcendence of the self through ice—a becoming-timeless demon, entering into a dance of geological time.

The work of British science fiction writer J.G. Ballard does a thorough, if exhausting job of theorizing a death drive toward the inorganic via the technological (*Crash* [1973] being regarded as his definitive becoming-machine statement). Ballard's writings are obsessed with all kinds of minerals, mostly solids: "The Cage of Sand" (1962), "The Terminal Beach" (1964), *The Drought* (1965), *The Crystal World* (1966), *Concrete Island* (1974), and *High Rise* (1975). These works exude a sense of desiccation and aridity, a world slowly drying up. Ballard's characters—consciously styled ciphers, "defined usually by little more than their profession and a few rags of memory" and generic, dull-sounding, and subtly ironic surnames ("Maitland," "Laing," "Vaughn")—are to be found drifting amidst the drying ruins, waiting for death.[21] In "The Terminal Beach," Traven finds himself in a nuclear weapons testing site, following the death of his wife and child, living out his last days in the midst of human industrial constructions—ruined bunkers and blocks in the process of turning into sand. In "The Cage of Sand" (which predates by seven years the moon landing), three protagonists (Bridgman, Travis, and Louise Woodward) eke out a strange terminal existence in a cordoned-off zone that has been contaminated with noxious Martian sand. By day, they hide from squads of wardens seeking to evict them, and by night, they watch the spectacle of orbiting spacecraft wrecks containing the bodies of doomed astronauts—floating graves in space.

It is Ballard's *The Crystal World* that fully realizes the becoming-mineral fantasy. In an unnamed country in Central Africa, a process of crystallization has begun to occur that produces a bejeweled forest that beckons and enchants those who step among its gleaming boughs, charming humans to fuse with its hardening growths: an Orientalist, colonialist death drive. This "jeweled twilight world" offers the seduction of terminal calm, a slipping back into the quiescence of the inorganic, back towards the slower rhythms of geological time.[22] The crystallizing forest thus presents a palliative to a humanity, understood as viral planetary aberration. The "crystalline trees," "jeweled casements," and "lattice of prisms through which the sun shone in a thousand rainbows, the birds and crocodiles frozen into grotesque postures like heraldic beasts carved from jade and quartz," offer the seductive fantasy of the inorganic as a simpler way of life, a dimension where the unalterable rules of the physical world govern untroubled.[23]

The post-war text that directly ties becoming-mineral with the nuclear bomb is Kurt Vonnegut's *Cat's Cradle* (1963). This cautionary tale reads Freud's death drive politically, as an irresponsible, open-armed embrace toward the inorganic via the obliteration of humanity and all organic life. This occurs when humans (hungry for domination and imperialism) tamper with the eco-materiality of the real at the atomic level, release the physical from its temporary prison, and—engendering an atomic apocalypse followed by an eternal nuclear winter—incite a new Garden of Eden that blooms, not with sickness and mutation but with the pure mechanics of the mineral. *Cat's Cradle* recounts the releasing of "ice-nine" into the world by a "father of the atom bomb." The ice-nine compound causes all water on Earth to turn to crystal as it is made to "stack and lock in an orderly, rigid way," falling from the skies as "hard hobnails of *ice-nine*," rapidly transforming the entire planet into a heaving and then quiescent ball of rock.[24] Everyman protagonist Jonah, after hiding out the catastrophe, ventures forth to behold a crystal world—an endless winter, humanity's irreversible tomb: "There were no smells. There was no movement. Every step I took made a gravelly squeak in blue-white frost. And every squeak was echoed loudly. The season of locking was over. The earth was locked up tight. It was winter, now and forever."[25]

Deleuze and Guattari similarly politicize the death drive, engaging Freud's development of the concept in *Civilization and its Discontents* (1930) as the aggression produced by the repressions necessary to form societies. For Deleuze and Guattari, the death drive is merely one function of the system of desiring-machines, not an end-point outside of it. The Earth is not visualized as cold and gravely inanimate, but as marshy and fecund. It is an original, territorial "megamachine" (the term is Lewis Mumford's) that permits production itself: a "great unengendered stasis."[26] Together this primitive territorial machine and its "immobile motor" form an original unity replaced by the spurious unity of the State: "the full body is no longer that of the earth, it is the full body of the Despot, the Unengendered, which now takes charge of the fertility of the soil as well as the rain from the sky and the general appropriation of the productive forces."[27] To the tune of a naturalizing Freudian death song (*eiapopeia*), the state is that which biopolitically regulates life and death—the "Death-State," as Eugene W. Holland puts it. It is under nationalistic capitalism that the death drive fulfills its function as a mechanism for stemming surplus production and routing excess back into the system: "bombs are the perfect capitalist commodity and an ideal solution to capital's notorious crises of overproduction, inasmuch as they blow up and immediately call for the production of more bombs to replace them."[28]

BM's exaltations of total war, atomic annihilation, and nuclear winter engage the ideological, technological, and geological dimensions of the capitalist state as a death machine. Impaled Nazarene's "Total War – Winter War," on their 1994 *Suomi Finland Perkele* (an album which playfully traffics in and parodies nationalistic themes and war imagery) reprises Industrial artist NON's song "Total War": "Yes we want total war! Yes we want fucking war!" Norwegian IBM band V:28 have based a trilogy of albums on nuclear apocalypse (including songs "The Brightest Light," "Unleash The Energy," "A Prophecy

Written In Uranium," "The Purifying Flames," "As The Sky Opens," "Dead Men's Choir," "World Wide Bombing Day," "Desert Generator," and "Can You See The Light Now"). In "Shut It Down" (on their 2007 album *VioLution*), V:28's vision of total nuclear war as a final shutting down of the machine of the world appears with chilling clarity. Accelerated guitar riffs recreate a race towards destruction as the lyrics describe a total shut-down: "No need to breathe / No need to live / To ignite the hate / To destroy the world . . . No history to preserve / No life to remember / No name to honour / No death to glorify / Shut it down."[29] The world as machine is being turned off.

The "doomsday machine," popularized by Stanley Kubrick's *Dr. Strangelove* (1964), reappears envisioned through BM's depressive thinking in UK band Skaldic Curse's album title *World Suicide Machine* (2009), whose cover features the symbol of a bomb within a cog against a dreary backdrop of red and black ruins. In cybernetic BM act Aborym's *With No Human Intervention* (2003), the world itself has become a vast, mechanized, death machine: we are the "Chernobyl Generation." Aesthetically, IBM substitutes the inverted crosses and spidery logos of traditional BM with radiation signs and industrial fonts.

"Two Variants Of The Same Machine": Industrial Black Metal

Though Ballard professed to having no interest in music and to never having purchased a musical recording, he is very dear to the Industrial community.[30] His world is one where the individual is crashed by the architectural machine—a vertical world of steel and glass, the human severed from the Earth. The field of biopolitics (given prominence by Michel Foucault in the mid-1970s), studies the ways in which we in late modernity accept, regulate, and disavow socially sanctioned, industrially-organized death. Highlighting the causalities of car death at home and colonial war abroad, Deleuze and Guattari write, "the Algerian war doesn't kill more people than weekend automobile accidents, planned death in Bengal, etc.)."[31] "Our age is the one in which a holiday weekend produces more victims on Europe's highways than a war campaign,"[32] adds Giorgio Agamben, speaking to the banality of violence that colors the fabric of our mechanized lives. Ballard himself makes a similar point: "About [44,000] people a year are killed on the roads in America. Of course, every death is deplored, but collectively it's manslaughter on a gigantic scale . . . tolerated as part of the price to be paid [for] the sort of lives we've opted for."[33]

Industrial music offers a self-conscious tool for coming to terms with the Death State. For ears living night and day amidst industrial noise (the whine and judder of construction site jackhammers and drills; the roars, grunts, and wheezing of garbage collection trucks; the vicious sneer of leaf-blowers; the crushing shrieks and squeals of the subway; and the incessant grind, whirr, and screech of moving and stopping traffic), Industrial Noise "music" articulates two mutual and dialectical functions. It sarcastically rhapsodizes and scathingly mocks the living death of post-war industrial society: the critiques of medical science (SPK), the pharmaceutical-industrial complex and mass slaughter of animals (Skinny Puppy), neo-fascistic nationalism (NON, Laibach, Ministry), and terminal urban *ennui* and soul death (Godflesh, Nine Inch Nails). But, it also arguably serves the function of assuaging the machine world, as its disjointed and alienating swathes of noise and repetitive and mechanical rhythms are made pleasant, propagating trance-like qualities.[34]

Industrial and BM might, at first glance, seem quite unsuitable bedfellows: BM celebrates and conjures the primordial, chaotic, earthen (chthonian and telluric), wild, bestial, and primitive.[35] It sings of—and enters into—the craggy, fantastical, pseudo-historical, medieval, frozen-over, ritualistic, Sadean dungeon, incantatory, blasphemic and vampiric, horrific, tomb, graveyard, and crypt. By contrast, Industrial music colonizes, describes, replicates, and de/re-territorializes the mechanical and machinic, clinical, compressed, and automatic, the enclosed, sterile (and contaminated) spaces of the factory floor, lab, hospital, power station, and nuclear generator. Both however, at a closer look, share a critical relationship and aversion to the industrial present—expressed through distortion, dissonance, and mockery. BM shuns this world by swooping off into the woods and envisaging a pre-industrial epoch of orcs, Vikings, and demonic forest dwellers. Industrial music faces machine society by tending its ear close to the hum and roar and grind of the factory's machinery in motion, exaggerating its features into a totalizing factory world. BM is wild and satanic; Industrial is cold and clinical. But both are rife with black humor, evil glee, and sardonic angst. Both are entranced genres: Industrial enters into the repetitive and percussive logic of rhythmic machinery—the engine and motor, the fuzz and static of transmission; BM pounds out its rhythms from the hum and the whirr of forest winds and glacial storms—but it does so *through machinic noise*, which it disavows and animates with Dionysian spirit.

Though the cross-pollination between Industrial and BM has not had anywhere near the fortune of that between, say, BM and classical music, it has nonetheless produced a substantial body of work and a handful of canonical releases, establishing a rapidly developing identifiable aesthetic and an open field.[36] IBM is not peripheral to BM, but arguably quite central to it. Burzum's man-alone with (drum) machine stance, replicated by every one-man BM band since, is central to the IBM tradition. Satyricon and the Moonfog label pursued an openly Industrial aesthetic during the late '90s and early '00s, with standout releases from Dødheimsgard and Thorns, not to mention Satyricon's own development from pagan/medieval themes, imagery, and sounds (for example, their albums *Dark Medieval Times*, *The Shadowthrone*, and *Nemesis Divina*) to a more clinical and cold Industrial aesthetic (from *Rebel Extravaganza* onwards), Electronica and Remix dabblings, and the services of Industrial-friendly producer Jeff 'Critter' Newell on 2002's *Volcano*. IBM introjects and blackens the Industrial genre, and takes BM to places it never thought possible: the mechanical future of robot and cybernetic science fictions, in which the machine has replaced (or threatens to replace) the human as the dominant species; *The Terminator* and *The Matrix* franchises, which re-imagine the world as vast and grim total industrial landscape.[37] IBM conceives of a world returned to its function as mechanism, shorn of human consciousness's critical or ethical faculties. What is left is consciousness as recording and transmitting device. IBM reinscribes the promise of total human annihilation, extant in (traditional) BM, to produce a post-apocalyptic scenario through the industrial language of the breakdown of the social machine and the collapse of the body politic.[38]

THE HUMAN COMPLETION PROJECT

Oslo quintet Red Harvest (named after a 1929 murder-filled Dashiell Hammett novel) assimilate and blacken Industrial's critique of humanity's onward mechanization unto obliteration, to portray a map of alienated inner consciousness in the service of colder external negotiations of the return to the inorganic posthuman. Their work (which includes 2000's *Cold Dark Matter*, 2002's *Sick Transit Gloria Mundi*, 2004's *Internal Punishment Programs*, and 2007's *A Greater Darkness*) imagines a drive toward the terminally mechanical and becoming-machine—a predicament to be met with both resistance and capitulation, with assimilation into the new machine order both a condemnation to human hell *and* a release from the prison of individual subjectivity, alienated from the mechanisms of the universe. Becoming-machine, or inorganic, is becoming once again part of the fabric of the universe. Red Harvest's IBM thus depicts a scenario in which we are privy to vitalism engulfed by mechanism: swallowed up, assimilated, and locked into grid-like workings of the universe as "Mekanizm."[39]

Sonically, Red Harvest are appropriating the relentless drum machine and guitar work of Justin Broadrick's Godflesh—blackening and accelerating the British duo's staccato blocks of riffage and laconic melancholy to focus on the industrial world as a ruin and end-point. In Godflesh, the human is subsumed into the machine as an act of spiritual transubstantiation: an "all-consuming rite of subjugation," as Jonathan Selzer puts it.[40] Godflesh's music (*Streetcleaner*, *Selfless*, *Slavestate*) reflects the desolation of the post-war failure of heavy industry, economic decline, and social anomie in the post-industrial wasteland of Birmingham and the North of England: Broadrick's songs are ironic hymns to the fate of the human within the machinic model, by definition faulty. Splicing Godflesh with Neurosis's tribal tattoos and melancholic (yet liberationist) perspectives on the reduced space of the human within the wider perspective of cosmic time, and Fear Factory's robot apocalypse lyrical scenarios, Red Harvest's music jitters—neurotically scraping, grinding, and mechanically chugging—never quite reaching catharsis. "The Itching Scull" (2000) seeks and finds the mechanical within the human skull, akin to Christopher Conte's "Miniature Biomechanical Skull" sculpture (2004), while Red Harvest's "Godtech" (2002) proffers a world worthy of the death-industrial skull aesthetics of artist Joachim Luetke, whose gothic industrial-mechanic tableaux have graced Dimmu Borgir albums:

> In a world controlled by machines
> Humans identify with machines
> Rather than regaining control over their lives.
> Godtech, the next step in evolution
> A superior being
> Using human plants as sensory organs
> It's the end of the world as we know it
> Digital life, bio-mechanical hell
> Transhuman express
> This is where you cry out.[41]

The human has become a function of machine reproduction, the world has become a conjunction of mechanized desiring machines; the human and world are now clearly linked to one another through flows. There is no separation between the organic, inorganic, machine, human, or animal: the human is an appendage of the machine. As per the words of Marshall McLuhan, the human has become the "sex organs of the machine world, as the bee of the plant world."[42] But consciousness and self-awareness persist: the human may awake from this grid through an act of will (*The Matrix*), to castrate machine reproduction—that which Mark Fisher terms the "gothic propagation" of mechanical reproduction, sex and organic death supplanted by the sexless reproductions of inhuman industrial capitalism. Human subjectivity is produced through a traumatic awakening into the machine world: the powerlessness of the human in the face of the capitalist socio-economic "machine" is rendered through the conceptual paradigm of the robot grid into which the human is assimilated, from which it dreams and fights to awaken.

Red Harvest's (the "Red" is human flesh and blood harvested for machine consumption/reproduction) "Death in Cyborg Era" (2000) describes this predicament in terms of existential confusion: "I am lost in a world I cannot understand / Technologies of vision / Technologies of death / Reconstruction / Reproduction." What is required of the contemporary subject is submission to the machine. Here is where masochism becomes the assuaging tool of machine culture, teaching us to enjoy and find pleasure in our imprisonment. As noted by John K. Noyes's *The Mastery of Submission: Inventions of Masochism* (1997), the paradigms of discipline and punishment identified by Foucault are but submissive adaptations to the rigors of the technological and the strictures of machine society. The human body bent "out of shape" to accommodate its mechanical yoke—whether factory, cubicle, car, or laptop. Red Harvest's *Internal Punishment Programs'* title track trains its eye on this form of submission: "A state of complete servile obedience / What have I become? / Perverted loyalty: totalitarian conformity control reindoctrination programs progress / What have I become? Systematic elimination."[43] The individual is interpellated into the new world machine order as feed for its machinery, meat fed into grinding caverns of systematized capital flow: "New world disorder / Meltdown of the human lap-top / You are born into this world / To protect and serve / Feed the golden vacuum of machinery."[44] We reproduce, as food for the machine, to propagate its mechanisms. As Nick Land puts it, "capital is a social suicide machine . . . compelled to advantage its assassins."[45]

By the time of their final album *A Greater Darkness* (2007), Red Harvest's vision of mechanized futurities has run out of steam, blown out, and washed up. What remains is almost bucolic: a dead world in which even the machines have tired of endless, senseless, and sexless reproduction. The album sounds sedated, cracked, and faltering. Armageddon has proved to be a thunderstorm: the realm of the natural impinges and threatens. Machines rust, rot, and grind to a halt as the larger system, the "greater darkness" of the machine of the world, reclaims and takes over. As for Norway, the discovery of oil and gas in the North Sea since the sixties has made it a rich country: the seventh-largest exporter of crude oil in the world. While BM dreams of a clean world of ice, disavowing its nation's subterranean fortune, IBM smears, like corpse paint, those icy fantasies with oil and grime.

BIZARRE COSMIC INDUSTRIES

In "AEP (Advanced Evolutionary Progression)" (2002), Red Harvest confirm we are doomed to remain earthbound, in struggle with the process of the machinification of the human—suggesting that the gaze attuned to the stars, so prevalent in BM, is a sham. They do so by putting to music part of a speech by wide-eyed Heaven's Gate cult leader Marshall Applewhite, who persuaded his congregation to join him on the passing comet Hale-Bopp (the cult committed a forty-member mass suicide in Santa Fe, California on March 19, 1997): "Last Chance to evacuate the Earth / It's gonna be recycled / Wiped clean, washed over / Your only chance / Get off the planet, now!"[46] Black Metal has a track record of gazing at the sky, the moon and the stars: at blazes in the Northern sky, moons freezing or in the Scorpio, and demons circling in time above time. IBM builds ships to go there, setting in motion paradigms of the alien and the cosmic, reaching out beyond the blackening planet, and conceptualizing music as transmission beyond the human.

Norwegians Dødheimsgard articulate this uplifting trajectory, specifically on their magnum opus *666 International* (1999). The album looks two ways: back in time towards the theological satanic, and outwards towards the global/planetary and cosmic posthuman. The cover art depicts what looks like an abattoir, with blood pooling into a drain, yet (enhanced by spherical line graphs) it also conjures to mind an airport lobby, offering departures to the unknown—beyond the death of the human. Eschewing the regular black and white corpse paint favored by BM acts, Dødheimsgard (*Død*=death, *heim*=home, *gard*=mansion) appear as a multicolored face-painted band of posthuman, necro-cosmic technopriests (Mr. Fixit, Apollyon, Aldrahn, Czral, Magic Logic). Warped beyond humanity by the nuclear fire, Dødheimsgard call in an incantatory act upon the physical elements, invoking the "glorious destruction" of ion storms to bring about apocalyptic destructions.

Dødheimsgard's music, which springs from a scene we might call "Carnivalesque BM" (including such artists as Ved Buens Ende, Arcturus, Fleurety, Solefald, Source of Tide, and Covenant/The Kovenant), here channels and recasts Skinny Puppy's juddering, cautionary bio-industrial tale as the celebratory, bizarre carnival of William Burroughs-esque cosmic pirates reaching out towards new forms of death and life in space.[47] Their mangled electronic beats, haunting synths, and off-kilter rhythms do battle with BM riffage, Progressive Rock tendencies, and atonal, distorted chants and lamentations. Dødheimsgard's restless glitchiness and abrupt transitions privilege rupture, palette shift, and multiplicity over grey uniformity, drone, or flow.

Dødheimsgard's lyrical content assembles surreal and postmodern works of bricolage, bridging Vedic appeals to calm through total destruction with nihilistic exultations of chaos and violence and the primacy of the primordial maelstrom as the antidote for corrupt modernity. In "Shiva Interfere" Dødheimsgard disrupt linear time to conjure an end to binarism, offering an example of science fiction interplanetary travel through the prism of Orientalist xenotheology. The traditional Norse gods have now made way for more esoteric and invented divinities. Svein Egil Hatlevik (aka Logic)'s cascading keys usher in a dissonant, disjointed crescendo of recombining synthetic riffage, eerily mechanical beats, and harlequinized, angst-ridden, declamatory vocals:

> Glorious destruction
> Glorious creation
> Grimly folds with luminous elegance

Winged between the corroded amber
. . .
Directly from an ocean of flowers
Visual contact, planet B8----18
. . .
Oh you are crystalline, I say, you are made of pain
For only suffering can create such beauty
And only suffering can wipe out your tears.[48]

"Ion Storm" spasms and judders, smearing its toxic sonic phlegm across cosmic BM accelerationism. "Regno Potiri" flits between Trip-hop ambience, bursts of mechanized BM violence, and grinding Disco-metal, lyrically weaving a tale of grotesque and carnivalesque techno/fleshly/sadomasochistic/insectoid desire. "Final Conquest" glimpses once again at the crystal world with agony and desire: "Wonderful and spastic, wandering along and clenching / The climate of frozen time / Hideous and accurate with bare longing."[49] The album's closing track "Completion" defines the human perceiving subject between the binaries of storm and calm, seeking in the latter a destination: "As all is said, we cross the storm / And watch ourselves in pray / For this no longer a mutant that shivers / This is here to stay."[50] Beyond the total war of the end, humanity remains as ghostly echo.

The cosmic storm is Dødheimsgard's chosen paradigm in *666 International*—their incantatory work between the glorifications of the storm that is chaos, and the desire for the calm after the storm that is human consciousness—envisaging future techno-mutant perceptive states that will replace it. Stormy are both the primordial soup that precedes and engenders the organic turn, and the astronomic Armageddon that is the sun as red giant (swallowing and burning up the Earth). That most BM of philosophers, E.M. Cioran, similarly perceives the maelstrom as both a release from human subjectivity and a chance for renewal as inorganic material, not as cold mineral but as hot gas (or hot air):

Let us return to original chaos! Let us imagine the primordial din, the original vortex! Let us throw ourselves into the whirlwind which has preceded the creation of form. . . . Let everything be wiped out so that, surrounded by confusion and disequilibrium, we participate fully in the general delirium, retracing our way back from cosmos to chaos, from firm to swirling gyres."[51]

SPACE GRAVES

Bill McKibben's *Enough: Genetic Engineering and the End of Human Nature* (2003) objects to immortality projects, on the grounds that removing death (and thus giving rise to a new species, *homo permanens*) also removes the limit against which humanity defines itself. "Without [the limit of death, the deadline] consciousness would carry little meaning; it would have nothing to rub against, it would spin like a tire on ice," states McKibben.[52] This may be a problem for humans but not for "the robot men that spin off into the future," who will presumably have reconfigured their bodies into tougher material than flesh and bone to take on the duress of interstellar travel.[53]

The compelling narrative of outer space as humanity's grave and final destination is the subject of Arcturus's *The Sham Mirrors* (2002). To use the word "odyssey" to describe this voyage would be imprecise, as no return is sought. Instead, the voyage is endlessly outward, unto death. The album's cover combines negative images of rock, a spatial vista, and a model drawing of a section of the Apollo spacecraft. Inside of the album's booklet, debris of digitally scattered images foregrounds the skeletal protagonist of the dance of death. "Kinetic" begins by introducing the work in the form of a transmission from a civilization that is long gone, a message from the past (as all art is):

Welcome
this transmission
from a fallen star
Light has departed
from this black sun
But please put us on
to bring darkness down
from your head and home
Our enterprise a success
as return is no option
our eyes were removed
for our own safety
This distance too great
for you to hear our cries
nevermind take this lamp
we are beyond light
We learned so little
of inhuman culture
before disappearance
went right through us
The mothership
boarded by fools
we escape space
in order to reach
our destination

And if you are listening
please tell us about the time
where and when we exist
no more
For when you go
we go with you
via wormholes.[54]

Civilizations that have ended continue to travel across space and time in the form of transmission: our time is spent fashioning a message to communicate (to ourselves) that we were really here, and not mere ghostly figments of our imaginations. Geosynchronous satellites orbit the earth and speak back to us through transmissions.

The surface upon which *The Sham Mirrors* inscribes its epitaphic message is a negative one which covets the logics of antimatter and the black hole as escape hatches from the human: "This negative kingdom / hey horrible and white / the angels all stone / passing their years / hoping to be saved / from oblivion / by oblivion" ("Nightmare Heaven"). Unlike IBM that screams its message amidst the roaring furnace of machines gone haywire, Arcturus's vocalist Trickster G. Rex (Krystoffer Rygg) sings in clean soars, enunciating his words for clarity. The music is pristinely produced, triumphant, and melodic Progressive Metal, drawing from BM and consciously moving well beyond it. "Star Crossed" entrusts to time and space the message of our ending, producing the organic human as inorganic epitaph:

We
organic images
dissolving earth
Our future children
stare at us unfixed
from a residence of stars
in their sidereal ships
ho sailing beyond within
. . .
And our vision
goes backwards
. . .
All dreams end here
where our cries began
resounding in museums
of a world we believed neverending.

Outer space is a negative heaven that provides not the solace that there might be something "out there," but the end of humanity as communication, or transmission, to ourselves. It is the echo we seek and find in the silent music of the spheres. And, it is endless circularity which haunts also *The Sham Mirrors*'s final track "For To End Yet Again," which configures endings as endlessly cyclical—in a sing-song carnival dance. The transmission bounces back, and we are caught once again in the loop, shuffling backwards.

"In space no one can hear you scream," states the infamous tag line to Ridley Scott's *Alien* (1979). This is because sound waves need molecules lacking in outer space to transmit them. Electromagnetic waves, such as radio waves, on the other hand need no such molecules: to this point, the ghostly effect of astronauts communicating via radio. Humans have been sending out our own radio waves into the cosmos since the 1920s, waves which are now between 50-100 light years away. In addition, there are our own recorded messages to the stars—the Arecibo message (1974) and the Voyager Golden Records (1977)—which feature recordings of animal sounds and music by Beethoven, Mozart, Stravinsky, Chuck Berry, and Guan Pinghu for aliens to listen to at their own leisure when they receive them.

French band Spektr (who take their name from the fifth module of the Russian Mir space station, isolated after a crash) construct an aesthetic based on these spaceward communicative tendencies, fashioning Electronic BM as a form of black box of the human experience, a BM techno-hauntology. The ghostly static crackle, drone, and haunting hiss of their releases "Astral Descent," "Phantom Reality," and "Disturbing Signal" (*Near Death Experience*); "Hollow Contact" (*Mescalyne*); and "No Longer Human Senses" and "Nothing's Benn Worth Saving (The Procession)" (*Et Fugit Intera Fugit Irreparabile Tempus*) re-program, cut up, dissect, and patch back together Burzum's mournful drone with swathes of white noise and discombobulating glitches, to stand for humanity's necro-posthuman digital epitaph. After notions of Cosmic BM as open (yet terminal) versions of a post-humanity—blind, undead, and sailing through space in the new kind of half-life in operation ever since radio waves were first sent out into the cosmos a century ago—post-Industrial Electronic BM remains as echo, afterglow, and specter of humanity. Floating code, communicating with nothing but itself.

FADE TO GREY

Back on Earth (among the humans chattering about their end) there are discourses that articulate eco-destruction as the last acceptable form of sadism: the "rape" of Mother Nature or the Earth. Visions depict eco-apocalypse as one last, final orgy. Perhaps inspired by the Tom of Finland drawing "Fuck the World" (1972), which depicts a muscular man copulating with the planet in space, Swedish Crust-Punk band Driller Killer express their preoccupation with the perils of industrialization as a form of planetary rape by titling their 1997 album *Fuck the World*, and gracing its cover with a picture of the Earth endowed with a planet-sized vagina. On a similar note, Marduk's tank-fetishizing *Panzer Division Marduk* (1999) features the screed "Fistfucking God's Planet." But, it is Finnish necro-fetishist "nuclear metal" band Impaled Nazarene who specialize in articulating the end of the world nuclear Armageddon as a holocaust orgy of sex and violence. Their 1996 album *Latex Cult* depicts the total war of the end as hell-orgy, sexualizing BM's long-standing fascination with pure holocaust:

> Karmageddon warriors, possessed soldiers, We are back from the grave, it's a doomsday . . . Motor action phallus, 666 ways to die . . . The return of nuclear god, Alien militant, Doomsday machinery, Cybergoat war, alien Jesus will fuck your face, your soul, Hell on earth . . . Hammering down the law, this is goat war . . . Masturbating with a gun, vomit fire and blood . . . My semen is made of hellfire.[55]

The album's David Palser-designed artwork features a mummified head-cast of singer Mikka Luttinen plugged into a mechanical matrix of wires and phalluses: the devil has been encased within the machine. Impaled Nazarene's irreverent humor ("Motorpenis," "66.6 S of Foreplay," "Masterbator," and "I Eat Pussy for Breakfast") suggests the surrender to sexual Armageddon as an act of defiant, satanic laughter. Their previous album *Suomi Finland Perkele* (1994) paired the two songs "Let's Fucking Die" and "Genocide" as the ultimate in sadistic gratification, total genocide as also a form of terminally masochistic global suicide:

> Genocide—what we need is
> Genocide—all must die
> Scum being raped, scum being killed
> Scum is dying, I keep on laughing
> Genocide—it's the fucking
> Genocide—all must die.[56]

Sex-hellfire-apocalypse comes full circle to reanimate the primordial chaos—where individuality and differentiation between subject/object, self/other, and organic/inorganic are finally erased in a singularity.[57] In Vernor Vinge's 1993 formulation, the Technological Singularity concept (or Singularity, as it has come to known and popularized by Ray Kurzweil) is understood to signify the moment in which the intelligence of machines equals and surpasses that of humans. It is an event horizon in which distinctions between human and machine are erased. In this moment we will be one with the machine, alienated and split no more, finally joined with our prosthetic other. But, eclipsing this in the cultural imagination is another "singularity": the oneness of grey goo meltdown. The hypothetical grey goo scenario is what occurs when biovorous, self-replicating nanorobots (whose job it is to build structures at the atomic level) malfunction and consume the entirety of carbon-based material on the planet, reducing the whole world to irreversible sludge in a matter of days. Building on initial warnings sounded by K. Eric Drexler, who in *Engines of Creation: The Coming Era of Nanotechnology* (1986) popularized the phrase "grey goo" (and who now regrets it, given that it is increasingly the public's first conceptual port of call when thinking of nanotechnology), Robert A. Freitas Jr.'s paper "Some Limits to Global Ecophagy by Biovorous Nanoreplicators, with Public Policy Recommendations" warns that "Ecophagic nanorobots would regard living things as environmental carbon accumulators, and biomass as a valuable ore to be mined for carbon and energy. Of course, biosystems from which all carbon has been extracted can no longer be alive but would instead become lifeless chemical sludge."[58] Grey goo futurities portend machine-facilitated returns to an inorganic singularity, where all difference has been erased and the grey matter of fleshly human consciousness—generated yet troubled by difference, partition, alienation—is finally erased in a sleep of eternal sameness.

Grey goo is also arguably an analogue for the crash (car or otherwise): a totalizing traumatic event in which flesh and machine are mangled into a terminal oneness, a "new flesh" to use David Cronenberg's formulation of a Ballardian trope: "In his mind Vaughn saw the whole world dying in a simultaneous automobile disaster, millions of vehicles hurled together in a terminal congress of spurting loins and engine coolant."[59]

Underground music is rife with articulations of reality crash. First the totalizing convulsion, the instant carnival bizarre, and genre-splicing maelstrom (Metal, Techno, Noise, Free Jazz, Skronk, Improv), then the hybrids (Grindcore, Powerviolence, Digital Hardcore, Glitch, Illbient, Cybergrind, and Pornogrind). The erasure of distinction and difference in a momentous lurch, an irreversible movement characterized by the burst, spasm, convulsion, glitch, and bleep. The totality of the real is maggot-ized into an ouroboric, whirling vortex of mechanical fagocitation, a general "spazz": the juddering ejaculatory blasts and noise-storms of Sun Ra, Lou Reed's *Metal Machine Music*, Merzbow, Napalm Death, John Zorn, The Boredoms, Meshuggah, To Live and Shave In LA, Agoraphobic Nosebleed, James Plotkin, Atari Teenage Riot, The Dillinger Escape Plan, and Total Fucking Destruction—or the newer names Whoukr, ØØPart, Control Human Delete, Otto Von Schirach, Kusari Gama Kill, The Amenta, Gnaw Their Tongues, iwrestledabearonce, Tampax Vortex, and Venetian Snares.[60] An unspooling, a sonic mangling: the gleeful schizotic, erotic, grotesque, nonsense dance of matter in its totality, spazzing out of control. After this, the greyness: the static of Ambient BM: grey metal, the mournful slumber of a sea of grey. The fade-out aesthetics of Ambient BM: Ash Borer, Coldworld, and Locrian. The inhuman geological Ambient Drone exhalations: Lustmord, Deathprod, SunnO)))). The slow and endless drone of an ocean of mineral oneness . . .

NOTES

[1] Ryder Windham and Peter Vilmur, *The Complete Vader* (New York: Ballantine Books, 2009), 36.

[2] Dana Jennings, "An Earth Where the Droids Feel at Home," *The New York Times*, December 8, 2011, http://www.nytimes.com/2011/12/11/arts/design/cedric-delsauxs-photographs-of-star-wars-on-earth. html.

[3] This includes Polish Death Metal band Vader; the baritone, guttural and muffled qualities of Death Metal vocals, which arguably owe to Vader's voice; Dub-Metal band Praxis's album *Sacrifist* (1993), which (on tracks such as "Deathstar" and "Rivet") constructs a martial and militaristic Metal style consciously inspired by Empire aesthetics; Dimmu Borgir, whose albums have become ever more adept at channeling John Williams's triumphant scores; and the cover art of Vondur's Cosmic BM classic *Stridsyfirlysing* (1995) whose depicts a triumphant Darth Vader and stormtroopers.

[4] In *What Is Posthumanism?* (Minneapolis: University of Minnesota Press, 2009), Cary Wolfe takes issue with transhumanism, arguing that its "ideals of human perfectibility, rationality, and agency inherited from Renaissance humanism and the Enlightenment" (xiii), which are far from "Haraway's playful, ironic, and ambivalent sensibility in 'A Cyborg Manifesto'" (xiii), render it an intensification of the dogmas of humanism rather than a process for looking beyond them. Wolfe intends posthumanism (as opposed to "the posthuman") primarily as a conceptual framework concerned with what may follow and critique "humanism," rather than what may follow "the human."

[5] Slavoj Žižek, "Organs Without Bodies: Deleuze and Consequences: The Reality of the Virtual," *Lacan Dot Com*, http://www.lacan.com/zizbenbrother.html. By calling it an "old boring topic," Žižek seeks to trace a dichotomy between Terminator-style narratives of machines "replacing" humans, and Matrix-style ones that imagine how humans and machines may co-exist. The shift arguably represents a posthumanist recognition of, or capitulation to, the idea that life without machines has become an impossibility.

[6] Laurence Goldstein, *Ruins and Empire: The Evolution of a Theme in Augustan and Romantic Literature* (Pittsburgh: University of Pittsburgh Press, 1977), 5.

[7] Laurence Goldstein, *Ruins and Empire*, 5-6. Goldstein is here quoting Thomas Browne's *The Garden of Cyrus. Or, The Quincunciall, Lozenge, or Net-work Plantations of the Ancients, Artificially, Naturally, Mystically Considered* (1658). The text is available online at http://penelope.uchicago.edu/hgc.html.

[8] Nick Yablon, *Untimely Ruins: An Archeology of American Urban Modernity, 1819-1919* (Chicago: University of Chicago Press, 2009), 5. Here, Yablon is discussing Walter Benjamin's thoughts on ruins from *The Origin of German Tragic Drama* and *The Arcades Project*.

[9] Nick Yablon, *Untimely Ruins*, 289.

[10] Alan Weisman, *The World Without Us* (New York: Picador, 2007), 121.

[11] Timothy Morton, *Ecology Without Nature: Rethinking Environmental Aesthetics* (Cambridge: Harvard University Press, 2007), 181–197. The concept has already found application in the nascent

field of BM studies: refer to Black Metal Symposium II: Melancology, *Black Metal Theory*, http://blackmetaltheory.blogspot.com/2010/06/black-metal-theory-symposium-ii.html.

[12] Yablon, *Untimely Ruins*, 293.

[13] Alan Weisman, *The World Without Us*, 6. Žižek categorizes this vision as a definition of "fantasy at its purest," (Slavoj Žižek, *Living in the End Times* [London: Verso, 2010], 80) and a definition of the Lacanian gaze (the impossible ability to observe the mechanical goings on of the world as if we were not here): "witnessing the Earth itself regaining its pre-castrated sense of innocence, before we humans spoiled it with our hubris" (80). Weisman's ecological consciousness-raising is viewed by Žižek as a fetishistic romanticization of "nature" as categorical innocent. He suggests it is the "cessation" of industrial activity that "would cause a cataclysmic imbalance" (80), referring to the position of "an environmental scientist" as a "good counterpoint" to Weisman's argument. So it is not totalizing industrialization but radical ecology that, put into practice, would bring about the end: a position which looks like a perverse apology for industrialism. Benjamin Noys similarly refers to apocalyptic extinction narratives such as the Roland Emmerich film *2012* (Columbia Pictures, 2009) or the History Channel's *Life After People* (2010), which involve the erasure of the human from the planet as "fundamentally reactionary fantasies which can only imagine redemption of our fallen world on the condition that humanity ceases to exist, or is reduced to the 'right' number of the 'saved'" (Benjamin Noys, "Apocalypse, Tendency, Crisis," *Mute: Grey Goo Grimoire* 2.15 [April 2010], 46). As I hope is apparent in this article, I wish to consider apocalyptic extinction posthuman narratives from the perspective of the cautionary tale rather than that of the escapist and conservative fantasy. Disputing the rigid and exclusionary dichotomy between revolutionary politics and "green" liberal habits of everyday life (recycling, composting), surely the latter have a better chance of tending toward the former than their apathetic or cynical alternatives (in the struggle against the right-wing politics of deregulation, trickle-down, entitlement, and ecological plunder). Saying "no" to plastic bags can be a first step to legislating against them.

[14] Sigmund Freud, "Beyond the Pleasure Principle," *Beyond the Pleasure Principle and Other Writings*, trans. John Reddick (London: Penguin, 2003), 84.

[15] Sigmund Freud, "Beyond the Pleasure Principle," 101. The novels of Cormac McCarthy identify and desire the mineral. The unspoken, silent protagonist of *Blood Meridian* (New York: Random House, 1985) is undoubtedly the rocky Earth: the geological stage on which humans crawl and battle like insects. McCarthy's lovingly-crafted crags, cliffs, drops, ravines, valleys, and plateaus unfurl confident of their existence within a far vaster timeframe, as humans suffer the inadequacy of their limited shells. *The Road* (New York: Knopf, 2006) is certainly a narrative which reaffirms the value of the human in the face of a harsh and terminal becoming-mineral of the Earth, but it is also one that foregrounds the Earth as almost happy to return to an inorganic state, a richly grey, unbuckling of the yoke of the human and its irritating scratchings.

[16] There have been several attempts to equate Freud's death drive with the second law of thermodynamics: the law of entropy which "specifies that all forms of energy—for instance, heat—tend to dissipate within a closed system" (Frank J. Sulloway, *Freud, Biologist of the Mind* [New York: Basic Books, 1979], 406). A picture of the universe entropically running itself down emerges also in the fictions of J.G. Ballard.

[17] Dominic Fox, *Cold World: The Aesthetics of Dejection and the Politics of Militant Dysphoria* (Winchester: Zero Books, 2009), 7.

[18] Dominic Fox, *Cold World*, 48.

[19] Dominic Fox, *Cold World*, 56.

[20] Especially regarding their widely-mocked photo sessions which live on as internet memes, and their widely-parodied videos.

[21] Will Self, "The Ballard Tradition" in J.G. Ballard, *The Drought* (London: Fourth Estate, 2011), 2.

[22] J.G. Ballard, *The Crystal World* (Farrar, Straus & Giroux: New York, 1966), 111.

[23] J.G. Ballard, *The Crystal World*, 93; Locrian's *The Crystal World* (2010) fashions a strange and ominous glimmering Ambient BM world out of Ballard's fantasy.

[24] Kurt Vonnegut, *Cat's Cradle* (Harmondsworth: Penguin, 1963), 36.

[25] Kurt Vonnegut, *Cat's Cradle*, 168.

[26] Gilles Deleuze and Félix Guattari, *Anti-Oedipus: Capitalism and Schizophrenia*, trans. Robert Hurley, Mark Seem, and Helen R. Lane (Minneapolis: University of Minnesota Press, 1983), 140–141.

[27] Deleuze and Guattari, *Anti-Oedipus*, 146.

[28] Eugene W. Holland, "Affective Citizenship and the Death-State," in *Deleuze and the Contemporary World*, eds. Ian Buchanan and Adrian Parr (Edinburgh: Edinburgh University Press, 2006), 164.

[29] V:28, "Shut It Down," *VioLution* (Vendlus Records, 2007).

[30] Though seemingly unconcerned with music, Ballard's writings profess an obsession with transmitting and recording devices as mysterious and orphic portals into other perceptive paradigms—his characters tuning in or listening to ghostly recordings. For Baudrillard we are living in a time in which time has stopped, and are stuck in a loop replaying our own errors like a film, "rewind[ing] modernity like a tape . . . [c]ondemned . . . as Canetti has it, to the retrospective melancholia of living everything through again in order to correct it all" (Jean Baudrillard, *The Illusion of the End*, trans. Chris Turner [Palo Alto: Stanford University Press, 1994], 10).

[31] Deleuze and Guattari, *Anti-Oedipus*, 335.

[32] Giorgio Agamben, *Homo Sacer: Sovereign Power and Bare Life*, trans., Daniel Heller-Roazen (Stanford: Stanford University Press, 1998), 114.

[33] *J.G. Ballard: Quotes*, eds. V. Vale and Mike Ryan (San Francisco: RE/Search Publications, 2004), 239. Text and brackets originally printed in *Mississippi Review* (1991).

[34] In "Violence in Three Shades of Metal: Death, Doom and Black," Ronald Bogue puts forward the idea that, according to Deleuze, music "de/reterritorializes" sounds from the natural world in the process of staking our claim over a given environment, and that Metal (whilst not exactly imitating the sonic mechanics of the machine world) nonetheless produces "sonic analogues of the sounds, rhythms, and patterns of the modern technological lifeworld," attempting a "deterritorialization of the diverse refrains of contemporary industrial machine culture" (Ronald Bogue, "Violence in Three Shades of Metal: Death, Doom and Black," *Deleuze and Music*, eds. Ian Buchanan and Marcel Swiboda [Edinburgh: Edinburgh University Press, 2004], 100). For some reason, this track (maybe too merely reactive in Deleuzian terms) does not interest Brogue, perhaps because the genres he analyzes (Death, Doom, and BM) tend to disavow their relations to machinic culture, instead seeking escape in mythological and fantastic realms. Industrial music (by contrast) openly and consciously embraces its relations to the machine world, positing them as its principle raison d'être. Industrial music exists as a relation to machinery, a way of relating to, and staking out the claim of the human within that world. As if, in order to communicate with the machines (who have invaded) humans had learned to speak their language and sing to them, perhaps to placate their inexorable onward grind. A statement by Throbbing Gristle visionary Genesis P-Orridge speaks to this relation, by which Industrial music exists as an attempt to come to terms with the new machine world: "till then the music had been kind of based on the blues and slavery, and we thought it was time to update it to at least Victorian times—you know, the Industrial Revolution . . . When we finished that first record, we went outside and we suddenly heard trains going past, and little workshops under the railway arches, and the

lathes going, and electric saws, and we suddenly thought 'We haven't actually created anything at all, we've just taken it in subconsciously and re-created it'" (V. Vale, ed., *RE/Search: Industrial Culture Handbook* [San Francisco: RE/Search, 1983], 9–11).

[35] Benjamin Noys, "'Remain True to the Earth!': Remarks on the Politics of Black Metal," in *Hideous Gnosis: Black Metal Theory Symposium* 1, ed. Nicola Masciandaro (Seattle: CreateSpace, 2010), 110–115.

[36] Honorable mentions must go to early not-always-so-successful attempts at mixing Techno and BM, such as the work of Mysticum and Diabolos Rising/Raism, a collaborative project between Impaled Nazarene's Luttinen and Necromantia's Magus Wampyr Daoloth.

[37] See also Alejandro Jodorowsky and Fred Beltran's graphic novel *Megalex* (Los Angeles: Humanoids, 2000).

[38] Agamben describes how notions of the human organism/organization, based up until the present on notions of "becoming" (from animal to human), have now gotten stuck. Drawing from the Deleuzian critical apparatus, Agamben terms the discursive mechanism which produces the knowledge of human as beyond-animal the "anthropological machine." But now that value of the distinction has closed (humans are not only animals, but exist exploitatively and symbiotically through non-human animals)—the anthropological machine is grinding to a halt, is "idling." The human project is thus configured here as an obsolete machine that has ceased to function correctly, and is now awaiting something: substitution, (genetic) reprogramming, and machinic replacement; "[F]aced with this extreme figure of the human and inhuman, it is not so much a matter of asking which of the two machines (or of the two variants of the same machine) is better or more effective— or, rather, less lethal and bloody—as it is of understanding how they work so that we might, eventually, be able to stop them" (Giorgio Agamben, *Open: Man and Animal*, trans. Kevin Attell [Stanford: Stanford University Press, 2003], 38).

[39] The title of a song on *Internal Punishment Programs* (Nocturnal Art Productions, 2004).

[40] Jonathan Selzer, liner notes, Godflesh, *Streetcleaner* (Earache, 2010).

[41] "Godtech," Red Harvest, *Sick Transit Gloria Mundi* (Nocturnal Art Productions, 2002).

[42] Marshall McLuhan, *Understanding Media: The Extensions of Man* (New York: McGraw Hill, 1964), 56.

[43] Red Harvest, *Internal Punishment Programs* (Nocturnal Art Productions, 2004).

[44] Red Harvest, *Internal Punishment Programs*.

[45] Nick Land, "Making it with Death: Remarks on Thanatos and Desiring-Production," in *Fanged Noumena: Collected Writings 1987-2007*, eds. Robin MacKay and Ray Brassier (London: Urbanomic, 2011), 265.

[46] "AEP (Advanced Evolutionary Progression)," Red Harvest, *Sick Transit Gloria Mundi* (Nocturnal Art Productions, 2002).

[47] I have taken the title of this section from a Covenant song off their *Nexus Polaris* (1998), a galaxy-galloping high-point of Cosmic BM. Their 1999 album *Animatronic* (by which time they were known as The Kovenant), saw them pursue a Cyber-BM approach, looking to such acts as Rammstein and EBM for inspiration. Cyber BM has found adherents, though not major commercial success yet, in such acts as T3chnoph0b1a, Neo Inferno 262, Neo Cultis, oOo, Blacklodge, and Alien Deviant Circus. A brief mention should also go to the subgenre of Cosmic Electronic BM, represented by the Pink Electro BM aesthetics of Zweizz (brainchild of DHG's Hatlevik), and the Psychedelic Industrial BM of Fullmoon Bongzai from Greece.

[48] "Shiva Interfere," Dødheimsgard, *666 International* (Moonfog, 1999).

[49] "Final Conquest," Dødheimsgard, *666 International*.

[50] "Completion," Dødheimsgard, *666 International*.

[51] E.M. Cioran, *On the Heights of Despair*, trans. Ilinca Zarifopol-Johnston (Chicago: University of Chicago Press, 1992), 90.

[52] Bill McKibben, *Enough: Genetic Engineering and the End of Human Nature* (London: Bloosmbury, 2004), 163.

[53] Bill McKibben, *Enough*, 163.

[54] "Kinetic," Arcturus, *The Sham Mirrors* (Ad Astra Enterprises: 2002).

[55] "1999 Karmageddon Warriors," *Impaled Nazarene, Latex Cult* (Osmose, 1996). Pushing home the point, the special edition album comes in a metal tin.

[56] "Genocide," Impaled Nazarene, *Suomi Finland Perkele* (Osmose, 1994).

[57] This being BM, there are also those who understand apocalyptic singularity in racial terms: French/Italian quartet Ad Hominems's *Planet ZOG: The End* (Musique and Traditions, 2002) and *A New Race for a New World* (Undercover Records, 2003), abbreviated to ". . . For A New World" on the US Elegy Records double-album edition, which feature such tracks as "Auschwitz Rules" (abbreviated to "A. Rules"), "The Psalmody of Sub-Humans," "Nuclear Black Metal Kampf," and "Arbeit Macht Tot."

[58] Robert A. Freitas, Jr., "Some Limits to Global Ecophagy by Biovorous Nanoreplicators, with Public Policy Recommendations," *The Foresight Institute*, April 2000. http://www.foresight.org/nano/Ecophagy.html.

[59] J.G. Ballard, *Crash* (New York: Picador, 1973), 16. See Virus's *Carheart* (Jester Records, 2003), another Carl-Michael Eide (Czral) project, for an example of post-BM which places the automobile at the center of its concerns.

[60] Venetian Snares's aesthetic resolutely pursues this scenario's infinite recombinatory possibilities in the cover art for their 2006 album *Cavalcade Of Glee And Dadaist Happy Hardcore Pom-Poms*, which features cows torn apart by machines in the sky.

THIS IS ARMAGEDDON
THE DAWN MOTIF AND
BLACK METAL'S ANTI-CHRISTIAN PROJECT

Joel Cotterell

Rising concomitantly with the adversarial nihilism of Black Metal, discourses of darkness have characterised the genre's visual and textual aspects since its genesis.[1] And yet, Black Metal's focus on all things dark and nocturnal finds itself apposed with invocations (perhaps less frequent, though equally significant) *vis-à-vis* the genre's defining anti-Christian project of the Dawn. Working complementarily with satanic invocations of night and darkness, Dawn's role—as a sort of "light at the end of the tunnel" that night represents—is of tremendous import to Black Metal's ideological struggle. It is the goal of this article to situate the Dawn motif within this struggle. From this gained knowledge, we may examine at once how Black Metal may inform our understanding of the Dawn, and how Black Metal perspectives on the Dawn and its cultural weight might influence our approaches to Black Metal theory and ideology.

While the Dawn as a lyrical motif features prominently in the Black Metal canon, for the sake of clarity and in respect of this article's constraints, we will concentrate our analysis on two of the more prominent iterations of the Dawn motif: "Awaiting the Dawn" from Primordial's 1995 release *Imrama*, and Satyricon's "The Dawn of a New Age" on their

1996 LP *Nemesis Divina*.[2] Prominent, that is, for the artists' high profile in the international Black Metal scene and the centrality of the Dawn motif to the text's meaning. We will additionally consider Inquisition's "Strike of the Morning Star" (*Nefarious Dismal Orations*, 2007) and Nazxul's "Dragon Dispitous" and "Iconoclast" (*Iconoclast*, LP, 2009), for their significance as more recent works touching on the Dawn motif.

THE LUCIFERIAN CONNOTATIONS OF THE DAWN MOTIF

So that we can better understand the relation of the Dawn motif to the Black Metal paradigm in which we encounter it, we ought to briefly consider the role that Dawn imagery has historically played with regard to Christian theology. Dawn, for instance, is the traditional time of the Eucharist—a summoning of sorts of Jesus Christ. It is a time of beginning and purification, where light is shed, and confusion and darkness banished.[3] The parallels between this process of "purification" and the redemptive reputation of Christ are obvious: through Christ, purification; through Dawn, light.

Enter Black Metal, and with it the taking (or perhaps liberation) of the proverbial torch of cultural representation of Dawn. As is understood in both Christian and Black Metal perspectives, Dawn is that part of the day-night cycle that unfurls light upon the world. It is a time of rebirth, a(n) (re)awakening of thought and experience. The obfuscating darkness offered by the night is lifted, replaced by illumination and clarity. In this way, the Dawn offers liberation.

When working within the anti-Christian ideological project of Black Metal, to invoke the Dawn is to invoke the Luciferian. The brilliant rise of the sun, at once searing and revelatory, is an embrace of the forbidden knowledges that the coming of Lucifer—"son of the Dawn"—represents.[4] As we will soon demonstrate, because these Luciferian knowledges necessarily exist outside the bounds of divine approval, iterations of the Dawn permit the escape from, and the destruction of, Christianity's symbolic authority. As it were, we turn our back on the Father and Son with the rise of the sun.

It is instructive to reflect for a moment on the character of this rejection, that hailing the Dawn and Lucifer the Morning Star within a Black Metal context should be an anti-Christian act is unsurprising.[5] What is important in terms of this article's contribution to Black Metal theory is that we consider *how* this oppositional act occurs, and, in doing so, to better understand Black Metal's essential ideological character.

Black Metal poses the arrival of Dawn (and with it Lucifer) as a violent event. Inquisition hail a Morning Star that *strikes*, promising to "obliterate" the sons of Christ. It threatens to "exterminate them, annihilate them," leaving in its wake a bloodied and "inverted" world in which "our ways" (the ways of the Black Metaller) are claimed by the very acts of extermination, annihilation, and obliteration.[6] The stake of the Luciferian Dawn's arrival is not so much the establishment of a new order, but the upset and annihilation of the old.

Such an understanding of Lucifer (the Morning Star, herald of the Dawn) is taken up by Nazxul in *Iconoclast*. Reference is made in the title track and in "Dragon Dispitous" to a violent arrival of the Morning Star which will "shatter alabaster spheres" and "destroy transient temples," "joining to form an army / that no host ethereal can withstand."[7] Again, the Dawn represents for the Black Metaller a violent obliteration of transient, though outwardly, strong structures and systems.

As an aside, it is notable that the Black Metaller's relationship to the Luciferian Dawn is, in the majority of cases, passive—we witness the Dawn, we wait for the Dawn, we welcome the Dawn, etc. The Black Metaller may "join" the Luciferian Dawn's destruction or take action to speed its arrival (as in the case of Satyricon's *détournement,* discussed below); however, in the end the destruction wrought by the Luciferian Dawn would appear to be external to, and much greater than, the Black Metaller. It is beyond the scope of this article to interrogate the anti-humanist quality of this phenomenon, though it is an interesting point to raise in any case.

Having established something of a knowledge of the character of Dawn's arrival and the violence that accompanies it, we ought now to further explain the conditions/targets of the annihilation wrought by the Dawn so that we may better understand the real import of the motif *vis-à-vis* Black Metal's anti-Christian project.

THE DAWN MOTIF AND PRIMORDIAL'S "AWAITING THE DAWN"

"Awaiting the Dawn" is valuable in this regard as it provides an intimate account of the Black Metaller's pre-Dawn experience and, consequently, of precise phenomena whose Dawn-brought demise is anticipated with relish by the Black Metaller.[8] With the opening lines ("Lilith . . . my bride, a love of sin so deep / Wounds of lust won't ever heal") singer A.A. Nemtheanga's avatar quite clearly identifies these phenomena for the listener. The song's savage, heaving instrumentation combined with these lyrics indicates a frustrated carnal longing that possesses the avatar, causing him to "yearn," "weep," "writhe," and "twist."[9] Clearly, issues of obstructed or painful desires are at play here. It is with the reflexive question "am I to pay the wages of sin?" in the third verse that we begin to grasp the nature of the speaker's environment (also the potential casualty of Dawn's arrival). The line is an unambiguous allusion to scripture, whose significance is twofold. Firstly, it alludes to the existence of a Christian moral system which is imposed upon Nemtheanga's avatar—*voilà* the object to be annihilated by the Luciferian Dawn. Secondly, the avatar's question reveals the existing moral framework to be no mere source of guilt or shame, but a system that hangs a charge of death over the head of the sinner. Little wonder that the Nemtheanga's sinning avatar should await the Dawn, hail Satan, and obsessively ask of the "tidings" that Lucifer may bring—at stake is the Black Metaller's life! Whether or not the Dawn offers a new moral framework appears unimportant—the speaker may "turn my face to a new age" though outlines no blueprint for a replacement for the current order besides its absence. The value of Dawn for the Black Metaller as put forth by Primordial lies in its liberatory destructiveness.

THE DAWN MOTIF AND SATYRICON'S "THE DAWN OF A NEW AGE"

If Primordial draw on the Dawn motif as a promise of the future destruction of Christian moral frameworks, the use of the Dawn motif in Satyricon's "The Dawn of a New Age" represents the realisation of that promise.[10] Given that our analysis of Satyricon's invocation of the Dawn motif is lyrical in focus, we may preface our analysis by commenting on the fact that the song's lyrics are taken almost entirely from the biblical Book of Revelations.

Lyricist Satyr engaged in little surface-level textual interference, with any editing being mostly structural in nature, in order to forge a consistent lyrical narrative. Beginning with Revelations 6:8, the passage is a re-telling of the biblical prophecy of the coming of a "pale horse" and its rider Death. Accompanying Death is a black horse with a crowned, conquering rider who brings with him the unprecedented disfigurement of the world:

> And there was a great earthquake, and the sun became black
> as sackcloth of hair, and the moon became as blood.
>
> And the stars of heaven fell unto the earth,
> even as a fig tree casteth her untimely figs,
> when she is shaken of a mighty wind. And the heaven
> departed as a scroll when it is rolled together,
> and every mountain and island were moved out of their places.

Taken in its original scriptural context, the above text constitutes a foretelling of the End of Days—that is, the effective destruction of the profane world in preparation for the return of Jesus Christ. With Satyr triumphantly proclaiming in the song's introduction that "this is Armageddon," the lyrics foretell, however, of no messianic redemption and none of the divine purification or reward that might be expected to follow the biblical End of Times. In this way, this destruction described in these lyrics is at first glance absolutely congruent with Black Metal's violent and oppositional character. It is thus tempting to consider these lyrics unproblematically true to Black Metal's ideological core.

To do so would be easy, though in bad faith. As has been widely argued, we simply cannot hold a text up as a direct signifier-referent link—the text must be understood in terms of its relation to other texts.[11] In other words, we cannot neatly divorce "The Dawn of a New Age" from its scriptural roots. This puts us in something of a bind, however—there is now a great tension between Satyricon's affiliation with Black Metal's anti-Christian ideological project and the fundamentally Christian origin of "The Dawn of a New Age" as a fundamentally *anti*-Christian text.

We can resolve this tension, and in doing so better understand Black Metal's broader project, by considering Satyricon's paraphrasing of scripture (apocalyptic or not) as a sort of satanic *détournement* of Christian authority over this instance of cultural communication. Guy Debord defines the act and phenomenon of *détournement* as a device to render subversive ideas that "have congealed into respectable truths."[12] By creating a sense of distance "toward whatever has been turned into an official verity" (the idea of the end of the world as a precursor to the redemptive return of Christ, for instance), the device of *détournement* reveals the "official verity" in question as something that is not immune to or ineligible of being questioned. As a result, the violent removal of such a verity from its authority-granting context obliterates not only the verity's verity, but the coherence of the entire system which has permitted this verity to reign as true. The scriptural text (historically granted divine authority) appears in such a way that it is eminently recognisable as scriptural, yet sufficiently modified so as to be totally unlike any experience one could have in its traditionally "proper" biblical setting. Satyr perverts verse order by following Revelations 6:8 with Revelations 6:5—to which he adds a phrase of his own invention. Such lyrical intervention has the effect of distancing the listener and the text itself from the authoritative certitude of the text's scriptural origins, and in doing so dissolves this very certitude. The dissolution of certitude and authority is driven home by its pairing with savage instrumentation and vocal delivery.

Détournement, as discussed in Debord's *The Society of the Spectacle*, is a phenomenon whose very existence is corrosive to any type of sign system that finds itself assailed by an act of *détournement*—that is, it is not so much the act of *détournement* which undermines totalitarian sign systems but *the fact that such an act would be possible*. In Debord's words, "*détournement* founds its cause on nothing but its own truth as critique at work in the present."[13] Relating this back to Black Metal's anti-Christian project, we can see a similar anti-totalitarian phenomenon at work in "The Dawn of a New Age." When viewed as a blackened, satanic *détournement,* the song's assault on the *author*ity of its lyrics' source has the effect of undoing the totalitarian ownership of meaning that the invocation of scripture has historically legitimised. Satyricon's *détournement* can be read as a satanic revolt of the highest order.[14]

At this point we are charged with the task of explaining how Satyricon's satanic *détournement* relates to the Luciferian Dawn. For if Satyricon's satanic *détournement* has simply accomplished the destruction of Christian systems of authority (useful though this task may be), what manner of "illumination" has taken place? What sort of day does this Dawn bring?

We hold that it would be fruitless to search for a "replacement system" that we can label the "New Age" brought about by Satyricon's Dawn. What this iteration of a Luciferian Dawn represents—as in the cases of Inquisition, Nazxul, and Primordial—is quite precisely an absence of totalitarian Christian modes of thought and authority. Indeed, Christianity's self-perpetuating and self-legitimising authority is burned away by the satanic solar rays of this Luciferian Dawn. To expect anything to be left in the wake of the Black Metaller's Luciferian Dawn is to ignore the boundaries of canonical Black Metal's essentially *adversarial* nature.[15]

CONCLUSION

Common to all examined invocations of the Dawn motif is the idea of the "process" of Dawn as a violent destruction of Christian systems. Within a Black Metal context, hailing the Dawn—and Lucifer the Morning Star along with it—becomes a gesture of rejection of these systems' authority and the welcoming (or participation in . . .) their annihilation. It is hoped that our analysis of the role of the Dawn motif in Black Metal has illuminated its importance *vis-à-vis* the genre's anti-Christian project. We would particularly highlight the notion that Black Metal need not be restricted to discourses of darkness and nocturnality in order to remain true to its adversarial ideological roots.

NOTES

[1] Proto-Black Metallers Venom birthed the genre's name and its discourse of darkness with *Black Metal* (1982). From there, we witness a litany of darkness and nocturnality within the canon—with the appearance of bands and releases such as Bathory's "Nocternal [sic] Obeisance," Emperor's *In the Nightside Eclipse*, Darkthrone's *Under A Funeral Moon*, Burzum's "Dungeons of Darkness", Satyricon's *Dark Medieval Times*, etc.

[2] A search of *The Metal Archives* database retrieves over 400 songs bearing the word in the title. Consider also that this search excludes songs not featured on full-length releases: *Encyclopaedia Metallum: The Metal Archives*, http://www.metalarchives.com/search/advanced/searching/songs?songTitle=Dawn&bandName=&releaseTitle=&lyrics=&releaseType=1&genre=black+metal#songs.

[3] Elizabeth Stuart, "Exploding Mystery: Feminist Theology and the Sacramental," *Feminist Theology* 12 (2008): 232.

[4] Ronald F. Youngblood, "Fallen Star: The Evolution of Lucifer," *Bible Review* 14.6 (1998): 22–31, 47; Carel Rowe, "Illuminating Lucifer," *Film Quarterly* 27.4 (1974): 27 [24–33].

[5] As well as being commonly considered one of Satan's titles, "Lucifer" (as many have pointed out) is a name referring to Venus, the "Morning Star." The complex and evolving identity of Lucifer is discussed in the above-cited "Fallen Star" by Youngblood and L.T.I. Penman in "Repulsive Blasphemies," *Daphnis* 38.3/4 (2009): 597–620.

[6] "Strike of the Morning Star," Inquisition, *Nefarious Dismal Orations* (No Colours Records, 2007).

[7] "Dragon Dispitous," Nazxul, *Iconoclast* (Eisenwald Tonschmiede, 2009).

[8] "Awaiting the Dawn," Primordial, *Imrama* (Cacophonous Records, 1995).

[9] We speak of "carnality" in its sexual sense in this instance, though the apposition of "wounds" and "lust" suggests a blurring of any distinction between the "sexual" and the "fleshly" meanings of the term.

[10] "The Dawn of a New Age," Satyricon, *Nemesis Divina* (Moonfog Productions, 1996).

[11] Notably in Jacques Derrida, *Of Grammatology*, trans. G. Spivak (Baltimore: Johns Hopkins University Press, 1976), 158–159.

[12] Guy Debord, *The Society of the Spectacle*, trans. Donald Nicholas-Smith (New York: Zone Books, 1995), 145.

[13] Debord, *Society of the Spectacle*, 146.

[14] At this point we might address the concern that Satyricon's satanic revolt is granted too much credit—the church remains powerful, and Satyricon are far from the first group to attack Christian modes of thought and authority. The value of "The Dawn of a New Age" lies in its status as a noteworthy contribution to Black Metal as an anti-Christian discourse.

[15] This notion of Black Metal as an adversarial genre is discussed in Juliet Forshaw's "Metal in Three Modes of Enmity: Political, Musical, Cosmic," *Current Musicology* 91 (2011), 140–162, and built upon in Hunter Hunt-Hendrix's provocative essay "Transcendental Black Metal: A Vision of Apocalyptic Humanism," in *Hideous Gnosis: Black Metal Theory Symposium* 1, ed. Nicola Masciandaro (London: CreateSpace, 2010).

Made in the USA
Las Vegas, NV
20 February 2022